How to
INVEST
SUCCESSFULLY

How to
INVEST
SUCCESSFULLY
Second Edition

Felicity Taylor

Kogan
Page

For Len,
who had the idea
in the first place

First edition 1983
Second edition 1986
Both published by
Kogan Page Ltd
120 Pentonville Road
London N1 9JN

British Library Cataloguing in Publication Date

Taylor, Felicity
   How to invest successfully. – 2nd ed
   1. Investments
   I. Title
   332.6'78   HG4521

   ISBN 1-85091-234-3
   ISBN 1-85091-096-0 Pbk

Printed and bound in
Great Britain by Billing
& Sons Limited, Worcester

Contents

Introduction   **9**

Part One: What are the options?   **11**

1. National Savings   **13**

National Savings Bank ordinary account 15; National
Savings Bank investment account 15; Save As You
Earn 16; National Savings Certificates 16; Yearly
Plan 18; Premium Savings Bonds 19; National Savings
Stock Register 20; Income Bonds 22; Indexed Income
Bonds 22; Deposit Bonds 23; National Savings
Information Service 23; Points to watch 24;
Summary 24

2. Building Societies   **27**

Deposit accounts 29; Ordinary Share accounts 29;
Subscription accounts 30; Save As You Earn
schemes 30; Cheque accounts 31; Term shares 31;
Extra interest accounts 32; Special offers 33;
Index-linking 33; Points to watch 33; Summary 34

3. High Street Banks   **36**

Deposit accounts 38; Regular savings accounts 38;
Investment accounts 39; Large deposits 40; Points to
watch 41; The Banking Ombudsman 41; Summary 42

4. Gilt-edged Securities and Other Loans   **43**

British government stocks 43; Local authority loans 48;
Investors in Industry 51; Finance house loans 51; Zero
Bonds 52; Points to watch 53; Summary 54

5. The Stock Market   **57**

The Stock Exchange 57; Fixed-interest stocks 62;
Equities 63; The Unlisted Securities Market 65; The
Over-the-Counter Market 66; Traded options 67; Other

share options 69; Personal Equity Plan scheme 69;
Unit trusts 70; Investment trusts 76; The Stock
Exchange: Points to watch 81; Stocks and shares:
Summary 81; Traded options: Summary 82; Unlisted
Securities and Over-the-Counter Markets:
Summary 83; Unit trusts: Points to watch 84; Unit
trusts: Summary 85; Investment trusts: Points to
watch 86; Investment trusts: Summary 86

6. Life Insurance and Investment   **88**

Whole life schemes 93; Endowment policies 93;
Variable life plans 94; Unit-linked life insurance 94;
Switching 97; Income and other bonds 97; Life
insurance linked to building societies 98; Friendly
society bonds 98; Index-linking and insurance 99;
Points to watch 99; Summary 100

7. Pensions   **103**

Personal pension plans 103; Backdating pension fund
contributions 106; Annuities 108; Additional voluntary
contributions 110; Loanback 111; Points to watch 112;
Summary 113

8. Investing in Things   **116**

Commodities 119; Gold 122; Diamonds and other
gems 124; Currency 126; Antiques and
collectables 128; Property 129; Woodlands 132;
Small businesses 133; The IG Index 137; Summary 139

9. Special Cases   **141**

Investing abroad 141; Points to watch 146; Investing
for children 146; Points to watch 149; Investing for
people over 65 149; Points to watch 152

**Part Two: What you need to know about how
the system works**   **153**

10. Taxes and Investment   **155**

Income tax 155; Points to watch 159; Capital gains
tax 160; Points to watch 162; Capital transfer tax
(inheritance tax) 163; Inheritance tax: Points to
watch 165; Corporation tax 165; Stamp duty 166;
Value added tax 167; Covenants 167

11. Interest 169

Interest rates 169; How is interest calculated? 170;
When is interest paid? 172; How is interest taxed? 172;
Points to watch 173

12. Financial Advice 175

Investment advisers 175; Finance and the media 178;
Libraries 180; Share shops 181; Investor protection 181

13. Financial Jargon 182

Assets 182; Balance sheet 183; Bulls and bears 183;
Capital 183; Contango 184; Discount 185;
Gearing 185; Hedging 185; Index-linking 186;
Indices 186; Liquidity 186; Portfolio 187; Yield 187

Part Three: How to make your choice 189

14. Be Your Own Adviser 191

1. How much do you have to invest? 191; 2. How long
do you want to invest it for? 192; 3. How safe must
your money be? 193; 4. Do any limits on different
kinds of investment apply to you? 194; 5. How much
time do you want to spend on your portfolio? 195;
6. What kind of return are you looking for? 196;
7. How much tax do you pay? 198; What to put in
your basket of nest eggs 199; Where to find out
more 200; Useful addresses 201

Index 203

Introduction

How pleasant it is to have money, heigh ho,
How pleasant it is to have money.

A H Clough

It is a pity that the word 'investment' conjures up the notion of privilege, because it is no longer true, if it ever was, that you have to be rich to take part in the game of making money from money.

One thing that the government's privatisation programme has done is to demonstrate that far more people are interested in the stock market than any of the experts predicted, especially when it is made easy for them to invest in small amounts. So whether it is a legacy from a relative who was lucky enough to own her own house, or the 20p pieces you've been saving in the Haig bottle, it's worth spending a little time on making the best use of it.

Like most professionals, financial experts have a tendency to blind outsiders with science, and your first glance at a financial report may give you the idea that this is a mysterious world completely incomprehensible to the uninitiated. This guide sets out to explain the grammar of investment finance, so you can understand the language. Once you have mastered the language you can get much more enjoyment out of using it, just as you enjoy a foreign holiday more if you can communicate, however haltingly, in the local tongue.

When you've learnt the language, you can say what you like. And this book aims to give you all the basic information you need to make your own personal investment decisions – not what to do but the way to do it. As in most things, you are more likely to get what you want if you do it yourself.

I would like to thank all those who answered my questions so patiently. The moral is, when in doubt, ask, because people are always happy to talk to you about their own subject. And don't hesitate to get more than one opinion: don't forget that you are the customer, and the professionals are there to serve you.

Felicity Taylor
April 1986

Part One
What are the options?

There are three parts to this book; the first part which sets out the basic facts about different kinds of investment; the second which summarises some essential information about taxation and investment advice; and the third which explains how to use the information provided to make your own investment decisions.

In Part One, each kind of investment, from bank deposits and building societies to gold coins, property and woodlands, has a section of its own, where the principles are discussed and answers given to the following questions:

How safe is your money?
Are there any limits on investment?
How do you invest?
What return does it provide?
How is it taxed?
What types of investment are there?

There is a summary of the main points at the end of each section and some tips on what to look out for.

Chapter 1

National Savings

Most people don't realise that National Savings and the Post Office are two separate organisations, and that the Department for National Savings pays the Post Office a substantial sum in commission each year to carry out its business. People who run sub-post offices get this commission too. It ought to be a great advantage to National Savings to have this access through the innumerable post offices throughout the land to savers and investors, and for many children a National Savings ordinary account, usually called a post office account, is their first introduction to money management.

National Savings has changed quite a lot from its old patriotic voluntary guise, and has become a highly sophisticated investment operation. Although it has the image of being for the small saver, National Savings offers substantial advantages to most investors. People in the higher tax brackets tend to be very well aware of these, while small investors miss some worthwhile opportunities, because they don't know about them.

How safe is your money?
There's not much chance of the government defaulting on its obligations, and in the past you paid for that security through low interest rates which did not always compensate for inflation. Competition for savings has changed all that, and National Savings now offers a safe and profitable investment.

Are there any limits on investment?
Anyone can invest with National Savings, but there is usually a limit to the amount that can be invested in any one scheme, although you can invest in as many different schemes as you like. Like other institutions, the Department for National Savings changes the rules under which it accepts investments according to the financial scene. It does this by offering different *issues* of the various types of investment, withdrawing the old issue when the new one is introduced. Investments you may have made in earlier

issues of the same scheme, or in different schemes, are not counted towards the maximum for a particular scheme. In 1986 the 31st Issue of Ordinary National Savings Certificates was on offer, with the Third Index-linked Issue, and you could invest the maximum in these, even if you hold earlier issues.

How do you invest?
Almost all post offices, apart from the very small sub-post offices, will handle National Savings business, so there should be no problem in investing your money. The Department for National Savings is doing its best to reform the paperwork, so that application forms and leaflets describing the various schemes become easier to understand. You can also write direct to the headquarters of the various schemes.

What return does it provide?
The return on your investment varies according to the type of savings scheme you choose; this is explained when the different choices are discussed.

How is it taxed?
National Savings schemes fall into two groups. The first, which consists of National Savings Certificates, Premium Bonds and Save As You Earn, is especially favoured as the schemes are completely free of all tax. Profits and interest you receive from them are not included in any assessment for income tax, investment income surcharge, age allowance or capital gains tax. The higher your rate of tax, the better the return.

The second group, consisting of investment accounts, ordinary accounts earning over £70 interest, Income Bonds, Deposit Bonds and the National Savings Stock Register are taxed. The interest and gains you receive from them are paid in full, without deduction of tax, so non-taxpayers do not have the bother of reclaiming payments made to the Inland Revenue on their behalf.

What types of investment are there?
The range of investments is quite remarkable. At the time of writing there were at least ten schemes on offer, with new ones in the pipeline.

National Savings Bank ordinary account

Anyone over the age of seven can open an ordinary account at any post office doing National Savings business. (Children under seven can have an account opened for them but money cannot be taken out until they reach seven.) You can pay in cash (minimum £1) or cheques at any post office, up to a maximum of £10,000, and can withdraw cash on demand up to £100 on any day, though for cash withdrawals over £50 your book is sent up to head office for examination. You can withdraw larger sums by arrangement with the NSB Headquarters in Glasgow (Glasgow G58 1SB). The service is entirely free. If you have used an account at the same post office for more than six months, you can apply for a Regular Customer Account, which allows you to withdraw more cash at a time.

There is a free standing order service for regular payments not more than once a month. This would be an economic way of making small regular payments for hire purchase, for example. The Paybill service allows you to pay bills like electricity and gas direct.

There are two rates of interest. People with at least £500 in their account for the whole calendar year 1986 get 6 per cent interest for the whole year. People with at least £100 in their account for the whole year get 6 per cent per annum for each calendar month they have a balance of £500 plus. For other months they get 3 per cent. Otherwise, you get 3 per cent a year.

National Savings Bank investment account

Anyone can have one, but money may not be withdrawn from accounts held for children under seven, and you can pay in any amount from £5 upwards at any post office. The maximum investment is £50,000. You receive a much higher rate of interest (11.5 per cent in April 1986) which is not tax free, and you have to give one month's notice of withdrawal. Interest is calculated on a daily basis, and is paid on each whole pound for each day it remains on deposit, up to and including the date of the withdrawal warrant. Interest is credited to the account annually on 31 December. You can withdraw money only by application to the NSB Headquarters, Glasgow G58 1SB. The investment account is now one of the few investments that pay interest in full, without deduction of tax, so it is good value for non-taxpayers, including children.

Save As You Earn

Both the ordinary and the index-linked Save As You Earn schemes have now been withdrawn, although existing contracts will be honoured according to the terms by which they were taken out. The Department for National Savings replaced the scheme with Yearly Plan (see p. 18). Some of the building societies continue to offer SAYE schemes (see p. 30).

National Savings Certificates

There are two kinds of National Savings Certificate, ordinary and index-linked. Savings certificates correspond to the term shares or bonds offered by the banks and building societies. You promise to keep your money in them for a fixed term in return for a guaranteed rate of interest in the case of ordinary certificates, or for inflation proofing with the index-linked variety.

Ordinary Savings Certificates can be bought at post offices and banks. When you first buy some you will be given a holder's card with a number and this will relate to all future purchases of these and other certificates. National Savings Certificates are free of all tax. Each issue has its own terms, depending on how keen the government is to attract your money.

> *Example*
> The 31st Issue was launched in September 1985 and is sold in units of £25 with a maximum holding of £5000, which is in addition to any holdings you may have of previous issues. It offers a guaranteed rate of 7.85 per cent if you keep your certificates for the full five-year term, lower rates year by year if you withdraw the money early.

If you cash certificates in the first year you get no interest, just your money back. You can't withdraw the interest; it is paid in a lump sum at the end when you cash in the certificate. After the first year it is calculated every three months and credited to your total.

To get your money back you obtain an application form and an official paid envelope from the post office and send it to the National Savings Certificate Office, Durham DH99 1NS. You must give eight working days' notice.

Index-linked Savings Certificates are no longer Granny Bonds; they are now available to everyone. You can buy them in the same way as ordinary certificates at post offices and banks, and will have a holder's card – the same as for other purchases of savings certificates. They are free of all tax. Again the terms depend on how short the government is of cash, but the Third index-linked issue, for example, is sold in £25 units up to a maximum of £5000 per person (husbands, wives and children are all entitled to the maximum holding).

The £5000 refers to the cost price, not the index-linked value. Each month your investment is revalued in line with the Retail Prices Index. If you keep the certificates for one year you get back the amount you originally paid in, plus tax-free interest which equals the rate of inflation, plus extra interest at a guaranteed, tax-free rate. Each year the extra interest rate goes up and if you keep the certificate for the full five years you get the top rate, which, for the Third index-linked issue, equals 3.54 per cent per year over the five years. So if inflation remained at about 5 per cent for the next five years, you would get the following rates:

Year 1	7.50 per cent
Year 2	7.75 per cent
Year 3	8.25 per cent
Year 4	9 per cent
Year 5	10.25 per cent

If you cash in before the end of the first year, you get no interest or inflation-proofing. After the first year, you get the index-linked increase plus the extra interest calculated at the appropriate rates up to the time of withdrawal. Interest is calculated monthly from the date you buy, so a certificate bought on 10 January begins to earn interest on 10 February. Every year, on the anniversary of the date you bought the certificate, it is revalued to include all the index-linked increase and interest you have earned that year. Next year's interest etc is calculated on the new value.

The index-linked value is decided by taking the Retail Prices Index for the month you cash in and dividing it by the RPI for the month when you bought the certificates, and multiplying the purchase price of the certificate by this amount. However low the RPI falls, you always get back at least what you paid in the first place, plus the extra interest.

You cash the certificates by getting an application form and official paid envelope from the post office and sending it to the National Savings Certificate Office, Durham DH99 1NS.

You cannot take out the index-linked increase in the value of your certificates during the five-year term, leaving the certificates in to earn more, but you can withdraw some cash without losing all the benefits of index-linking. You look up the *repayment value chart* in the post office, and see how much £25 units purchased in a particular month have increased in value. If you need £300, and three years into the contract your £25 certificates are now valued at £31 each, you can cash in 10 of them to raise the money. You would not need to cash in 12 to get £300.

Quite often, people hang on to National Savings Certificates long after the repayment date has passed. This is not recommended, as the rate of interest paid has been very poor, unless the issue was specifically extended for a longer term. But the Department for National Savings now offers a General Extension Rate, which applies to all issues since the Seventh that have passed their repayment date. This varies according to the money markets. In April 1986 it was 8.52 per cent.

Yearly Plan

Yearly Plan replaced the SAYE scheme in 1984. It offers a monthly savings scheme in which you make regular payments each month for 12 months, by standing order. At the end of the year, you receive a Yearly Plan Certificate. You have to keep this for another four years to get the best interest rate. You can buy further certificates by continuing your standing order payments.

The minimum payment per month is £20, increasing by £5 a step to a maximum of £200 a month. You cannot change the amount you pay in during the year, but you can start buying new certificates at any time, as long as you are not paying more than £200 a month altogether. You don't have to count payments you may be making under other schemes, either with building societies or earlier National Savings schemes.

Yearly Plan offers a fixed rate of interest; the rate is guaranteed over five years, from the date you begin the scheme, whatever happens to other interest rates. All the interest is tax free. In December 1985 the rate was 8.19 per cent per annum tax free, if you kept your Certificate the full five years. So 12 monthly payments of £20, £240 altogether, would be worth £343.42 after four more years. If you cash it in in the first year, you receive no interest. You get 6.75 per cent tax free if you cash it in in the second or third year, and 7.5 per cent tax free if you cash it in in the fourth year or before the end of the fifth year. If you keep it longer than five years, you receive the General Extension Rate (8.52 per cent in 1986) paid on other National Savings Certificates (see p. 18).

Interest is calculated on whole months, beginning on the first of the month after the payment was made. So each payment begins to earn interest on the first of the month after it was paid in. The value of the Yearly Plan Certificate at the end of the first year equals the total of the monthly payments plus the interest they have earned. After that the Certificate continues to earn interest monthly until you cash it in. If you withdraw early, you will receive interest only on whole months, so it is best to pay in near the end of the month, and if you have to withdraw early, try to do it at the beginning of the month.

You can get application forms, including the standing order form, and full details from post offices. You send these in the envelope provided to the National Savings Certificate Office, Yearly Plan Section, Durham DH99 1NS. Repayment is by post only from the Savings Certificate Office, and forms are obtainable from post offices.

If you are considering this scheme, you need to be fairly certain that you can keep up the payments, especially for the first year. Otherwise, you might be better off with one of the other National Savings schemes.

Premium Savings Bonds

We all know that gambling is a mug's game, and in spite of their appeal premium bonds are no exception. *Which?* calculated that you have about one chance in a hundred of winning a prize if you keep £10 in premium bonds for a year, and about one chance in 12 million of winning the jackpot of £250,000. What's more, the Department for National Savings pays out only the equivalent of 7.75 per cent interest on the money invested in premium bonds as prize money. The odds on the Grand National are a bit better. However, that has not prevented the sale of over £1200 million worth of bonds, which just shows how addicted we are to gambling. Of course, the more bonds you hold the better your chances are, so higher rate taxpayers in particular may feel that premium bonds are worthwhile, in the knowledge that any prize they do win will be completely tax free.

You can buy bonds in the post office or bank. They cost £1 each, with a minimum purchase of £10, and you can hold up to

£10,000-worth. You have to keep the bond for three months before it is entered in the prize draw. Anyone over 16 can buy them, and they can be bought for people under 16 by parents, grandparents or guardians. If someone *under* 16 wins a prize, the parent or legal guardian has to hold it *in trust* for the child.

The amount of prize money is determined by the amount invested in Premium Bonds, and ERNIE, the Electronic Random Number Indicator Equipment, produces the winning numbers. The monthly prizes range from £50 to £250,000 and there are weekly prizes of £25,000, £50,000 and £100,000. The Premium Bonds Office write to you if you win a prize, at the most recent address they have for you, so make sure you tell them if you move. Forms are available at the post office. There are thousands of prizes unclaimed because people have failed to inform the office of their new address.

The claim that this is gambling without losing your stake money is not strictly true, as inflation affects Premium Bonds like anything else. If you have kept £1 bonds bought in the early 1960s and you cash them in now, the comparative purchasing power is about 12p.

If you want to cash in your bonds, you get an application form and official paid envelope from the post office or bank which you send up to the Bonds and Stock Office, Lytham St Annes, Lancashire FY0 1YN.

National Savings Stock Register

Gambling with stocks and shares is a little more profitable than gambling with ERNIE, and National Savings can even help you do this. Admittedly you are not risking much by investing in government stocks, which are all the Register deals in, but it's a far cry from the old-style National Savings.

The National Savings Stock Register is really a back door into the stock market. It offers the small investor a simple way of buying and selling gilt-edged securities, the government stocks that are its main way of financing expenditure apart from taxation. (Gilts are discussed fully on pp. 43-8.)

You can choose from a range of about 50 stocks, offering different interest rates, including index-linked gilts. The prices for stock are quoted for units of a face value of £100, but you can buy smaller amounts. When ordering stock you can either specify how much you want to spend, or order a fixed number of units at face value. The actual price depends on the market; you can get some idea of this from the daily reports in the financial press. All the necessary forms, with prepaid envelopes, are available in the post office, but you buy and sell by post, dealing with the Bonds and Stock Office, Blackpool, Lancashire FY3 9YP.

Anyone can buy stock from the Register, but amounts bought for children under seven cannot normally be sold until the child reaches that age. You cannot buy more than £10,000-worth on any one day, but there are no restrictions on the total amount you can hold. You can sell as much as you like at one time.

Interest is paid without deduction of tax, and it is assessable for income tax, investment income surcharge (1985-6 tax year), and age allowance. However, from 1 July 1986, when you sell gilts there is no liability for capital gains tax. The interest is paid to you half-yearly, preferably through your bank or National Savings Bank. You can have it sent to you direct, but that costs more.

There are three important differences from other forms of National Savings:

- Because stocks are bought and sold on the stock market you cannot know in advance what the price is for a £100 unit of stock.
- This applies when you want your money back as well. The price you get depends on the price prevailing in the market. It cannot be guaranteed. You cannot specify the day when you want your stocks to be bought or sold, and because you are dealing with the Register by post, there is always a time lag between the price you see in your daily paper and the price you get, or pay.
- There are commission charges on buying and selling stock, though these are generally much lower than you would have to pay a stockbroker, and very advantageous for small investors. Current charges work out at about £1 per £250 you spend or receive.

Although you can buy index-linked gilts on the National Savings Stock Register, you may not get the full benefit of index-linked value. (See p. 17.)

Using the National Savings Stock Register is an easy and painless way to begin dabbling on the Stock Exchange, though you are unlikely to make a quick killing.

Income Bonds

These were introduced by National Savings to attract investors who want a reasonably secure regular income rather than capital growth. You agree to leave your money in the scheme for up to ten years at three months' notice of withdrawal. In return you receive a monthly income at a high rate of interest (12 per cent in April 1986).

The interest is calculated on a day-to-day basis from the day you pay in your money, and is paid without deduction of tax. So for an investment of £5000 you would get £50 a month, £600 a year, if the rate remained at 12 per cent. The rate will vary according to the money markets; six weeks' notice will be given of changes. The monthly payments begin six weeks after you join the scheme. The income is assessable for income tax, investment income surcharge (1985-6 tax year), and age allowance.

The minimum investment is £2000; you can add to your original investment in multiples of £1000, up to the maximum of £50,000. You can withdraw £1000 at a time, but must leave at least £2000 in the scheme.

You can withdraw your money if you give three months' notice. If you keep the bonds for at least a year you will get the full rate of interest on withdrawal. If you withdraw during the first year you will get interest at half-rate. If you have been paid too much interest before you withdraw your money, this will be deducted when your capital is repaid.

Almost anyone can buy Income Bonds. Forms are available at the post office, and you buy by post from the Bonds and Stock Office, Blackpool FY3 9YP.

Indexed Income Bonds

A new development in income bonds is the Index Income Bond introduced in December 1985. Each bond costs £1000, with a minimum investment of £5000, and a maximum of £50,000. The bonds guarantee inflation-proofed income for ten years, starting at a rate of 8 per cent paid monthly, which equals 8.3 per cent a year. (This compares with 12 per cent being paid on the ordinary bonds when the new bonds were launched.) At the end of each year, the monthly income payment is increased in line with the Retail Prices Index (see p. 186). Other conditions are the same as for the ordinary income bonds.

Although the income will rise with inflation the capital invested will remain the same. This means that, although your income is protected by the bond, your capital is not. Most other index-linked investments (see p. 186) pay lower rates of interest but protect your capital.

Deposit Bonds

The Deposit Bond is designed for people who want to invest a lump sum and increase their capital. The bonds pay a high rate of interest, subject to tax, but the tax is not deducted before you receive the interest.

Interest is calculated on a daily basis, and is added to the bond at the end of each year, on the anniversary of the date it was bought.

The minimum cost for one bond is £100. The cost goes up in units of £50, and the maximum amount you can hold is £50,000, not including any added interest.

You must give three months' notice of withdrawal, and you can take out not less than £50 at a time. You can either withdraw the whole bond, or cash in part of it, as long as there is at least £100 left, including any added interest. If you cash the bond during the first year, you get interest at half the going rate.

Application forms are available at the post office. You can either hand one in over the counter, with a cheque, or write to the Deposit Bond Office, National Savings, Glasgow G58 1SB. The Bond Office will send you an investment certificate. Repayment is by post from the Bond Office. Forms are available at post offices.

National Savings Information Service

You can telephone National Savings for information about all its investments. The number to call is:

South: (London) 01-605 9461
North: (Glasgow) 041-649 4555 ext 2283

For recorded information about interest rates telephone:

South: (London) 01-605 9483
North: (Lytham St Annes) 0523 723714
Scotland: (Glasgow) 041-632 2766.

Points to watch

- Penalties are charged in many National Savings schemes if you don't keep to the rules, eg no interest in the first year if you withdraw early.
- When a new issue comes out, it may be to your advantage to withdraw what you have in an earlier issue, and re-invest it in the new one. Don't expect National Savings to tell you this, as it would be against the Department's interest.
- The investment account, paying 11.50 per cent in full, with few conditions and no loss of interest if you give notice to withdraw, is better value, especially for non-taxpayers, than a bank deposit account or most building society rates.
- Index-linked National Savings Certificates are a good hedge against inflation, and most people ought to put some of their nest eggs into this basket.
- When you pick up leaflets about National Savings at the post office make sure they are about the most recent issues; sometimes they are very out of date.
- Always compare what National Savings offers with the similar schemes offered by banks and building societies, before making your choice.

Summary

National Savings Certificates, Premium Savings Bonds, Yearly Plan

SAFETY	
Will the capital be repaid in full?	Yes.
Are the investments officially regulated?	Yes.
Is the capital protected against inflation?	Yes, if index-linked.
AVAILABILITY	Excellent.
METHOD	
How do you invest?	Through post offices, banks, postal applications.
Are there commission charges?	No.

Are there extra charges when you buy and sell?	No.

INCOME

Is income paid regularly?	No. Paid at end of term; none for Premium Bonds.
Is it guaranteed?	Yes.
Are there prospects for capital gains?	No. (Unless you win on Premium Bonds.)
Is the income high/average/low?	Average.

TAXATION

Is the return assessed for income tax?	No.
Is basic rate deducted?	—
Can the tax be reclaimed?	—
Is it assessed for age income relief?	No.
Is it assessed for investment income surcharge?	No.
Is it assessed for capital gains tax?	No.

Income Bonds, Investment Account, National Savings Stock Register, Ordinary Account, Deposit Bonds

SAFETY

Will the capital be repaid in full?	Yes, except for NSSR which depends on market price.
Are the investments officially regulated?	Yes.
Is the capital protected against inflation?	No, except for NSSR where it depends on stock market prices.

AVAILABILITY

	Excellent.

METHOD

How do you invest?	Through post offices, banks and postal applications.
Are there commission charges?	Only for NSSR.

Are there extra charges when you buy and sell?

No, except for NSSR.

INCOME

Is income paid regularly?

Interest calculated yearly or half-yearly. Income Bonds paid monthly.

Is it guaranteed?

Varies according to money market. Increases with inflation for Indexed Income Bonds.

Are there prospects for capital gains?

Only for NSSR.

Is the income high/average/low?

High, except ordinary accounts.

TAXATION

Is the return assessed for income tax?

Yes, except first £70 from ordinary accounts.

Is basic rate deducted?

No.

Can the tax be reclaimed?

—

Is it assessed for age income relief?

Yes, except first £70 from ordinary accounts.

Is it assessed for capital gains tax?

No

Chapter 2

Building Societies

The essential point for investors to remember about building societies is that they are not usually good value for people who don't pay income tax, because you cannot claim a refund from the Inland Revenue for the tax paid by the society before you get your interest. Otherwise, you can say that building societies are as safe as houses as an investment. They borrow money from the public to lend to people who want to buy their own homes, and they are one of the most popular ways of saving for small investors.

There are good reasons for this, the most significant being that when people are thinking of buying a house and hoping to get a mortgage, they often begin saving with a building society. If this means you, don't walk into the nearest building society branch on the High Street. Find out something about the lending policies of different societies first. You need to know whether the society you choose will lend money to the kind of borrower you are, on the kind of property you hope to buy.

Many changes have taken place in the building society movement in recent years, mainly due to competition from the banks and other lenders. Even more are likely when the new legislation promised by the government for 1987 enables them to offer a much wider range of financial services. There are many variations on the traditional building society account, so find out about as many as possible before you invest your money.

How safe is your money?
Building societies come under the aegis of the Chief Registrar of Friendly Societies who keeps an eye on their affairs and can intervene to prevent a society from taking unusual risks. The great majority of societies belong to the Building Societies Association. This has always given some guarantee of security because of the Association's entrance requirements, and its willingness to come to the rescue of members in distress. The BSA has now gone further and introduced a formal investment protection scheme, open to members and non-members. Most members have joined,

some non-members haven't. The proposed legislation has been criticised for setting up a statutory scheme which is in fact less generous than the BSA voluntary one.

Is there any limit on investment?
Anyone can invest in a building society, but there is no longer any statutory limit to the amount you can invest in one society. Each society can decide whether or not to fix a limit, and if so what it should be. You can invest in as many different societies as you like.

How do you invest?
One reason for their popularity is that they are easy to use. There are branches of several different societies in every shopping or business area. All you have to do is walk in with your money; there is very little fuss or formality about joining. They are not as intimidating as banks, not as busy as the post office. And they are open on Saturday mornings and normal shop or office hours.

What return does it provide?
Because of the keen competition for savings, most of the large societies pay and charge very similar interest rates. The smaller societies often offer higher rates, while non-members of the BSA pay extra to attract investors. You have to weigh that advantage against the loss of security involved in investing without the BSA's guarantee. If you do decide to take the risk of investing in a non-BSA member, it is a wise precaution to find out if they have joined the investment protection scheme before you part with your money.

Interest is normally calculated on a day-to-day basis from the day you pay in the money and is credited to the account twice a year. For term shares, and some extra interest accounts, societies now offer a choice of methods of payment. You can have it paid direct to you yearly or half-yearly, into an ordinary share account, or added to your original investment. You can also get the interest paid direct to you monthly in some cases, although you may have to invest a minimum amount, eg £1000, to qualify for this. The *Financial Times* publishes a table every Saturday giving details of the rates offered by the leading societies.

How is it taxed?

As explained on p. 158, the building society pays tax at a special rate before you get your interest, so if you are a basic rate taxpayer you have no more to pay. You can't reclaim any tax paid by the building society if your income falls below the tax threshold. On the other hand, the Inland Revenue can add your building society interest to your other income and claim extra tax if this brings your income over the basic rate band, or over the limit for age allowance.

What types of investment are there?

There are four main kinds of investment with building societies, which vary according to the length of notice you have to give before you can take your money out. The societies give their schemes a variety of names, but basically the schemes are as follows:

Deposit accounts

These do not get much publicity nowadays, as they are largely superseded by more profitable schemes. They pay a lower rate of interest than the Ordinary Share account, on the basis that if the building society runs into difficulties, the holders of deposit accounts have first claim on the money available to repay investors. As it's very unlikely that a BSA member would run into danger of bankruptcy, there's not much point in taking a lower rate of interest than you would otherwise get.

Ordinary Share accounts

You can open an Ordinary Share account simply by walking into a building society branch and paying in a minimum sum, usually £1. You can put in and take out money at most branches any time they are open, though you may need to give notice for large amounts or cheques. Interest is paid on the amount in the account for each day it remains there, usually on a half-yearly or yearly basis, and credited to your account. The interest rate was 6 per cent in April 1986, small societies may give 0.25 to 0.75 per cent more, and non-member societies might pay 1 per cent over this.

Subscription accounts
(monthly savings plan, savings schemes, build-up shares)

In return for promising to save regularly, you get a higher rate of return on your savings, at present 1.25 to 1.5 per cent over the recommended Ordinary Share rate. You normally have to pay in the same amount on the same day each month, at any branch or by post or banker's order. You can make withdrawals only from your own branch. Monthly investment can be as little as £1, up to a maximum of between £40 and £200, sometimes more. If you pay all the instalments on time, there may be a small bonus on the total amount at the end of each year. Some societies may have a limit on the amount you can invest in subscription shares.

If you need to withdraw some money unexpectedly, there may be some interest penalty, or other limitations, eg you may be able to make only one withdrawal a year, or you may have to leave a minimum sum in the account. Societies will often transfer your money automatically to an Ordinary Share account if you fail to keep to the rules of the savings scheme, rather than close the account altogether.

Save As You Earn schemes

Although some societies continue to offer a basic SAYE scheme, these are no longer as popular as they once were. The societies' own regular savings schemes may offer a better rate of return. However, SAYE schemes do have tax advantages over other building society investments, as the gains you make from them are entirely tax free.

Anyone over 16 can agree to save regularly for five years any amount from £1 to £20 a month, 60 monthly payments in all. At the end of that time you receive a tax-free bonus which equals 14 monthly instalments, so if you pay in £10 a month, you get £140 bonus at the end. If you leave your money in the scheme for another two years, not adding extra payments, the bonus doubles to equal 28 months' instalments.

This bonus works out at a rate of 8.3 per cent per year over five years, 8.62 per cent over seven years, calculated monthly. This is less than some other building society shares on seven-day notice were receiving in 1985, but the rate is guaranteed for the life of the contract. If you stop payments during the first year, you get your money back without interest. After that you get 6 per cent on what you paid in if you fail to complete the five years.

You can arrange for the payments to be deducted from your salary, either monthly or in four-weekly instalments, and paid direct to the society.

If you complete the five-year contract, and then decide to leave the money in to earn the seven-year bonus, but change your mind later on and ask for the money back, you will receive only the amount due at the end of five years, including the bonus. There is no allowance for the extra time you have left the money in.

Lump sum SA YE is an ingenious way of getting the tax advantages of SAYE out of a capital sum. Some building societies offer schemes by which you pay a lump sum equal to your 60 monthly contributions into a special share account. Each month the building society transfers one instalment to the SAYE account, while the remainder of the lump sum continues to earn interest in its own right. At the end of five years you have the SAYE contributions plus the bonus of 14 contributions tax free, but the interest earned by the lump sum in the share account is in effect an extra bonus, free of basic rate tax. You can leave the SAYE investment in for another two years and earn the extra bonus if you wish.

Even if you don't want to tie up a lump sum you may be able to do this by operating your share account so that there is always enough in it to pay the SAYE instalment. You can then leave the money on deposit in the share account, earning interest, up to the last day on which it is due in the SAYE scheme.

Cheque accounts

Carrying the war into the enemy camp, or sometimes even in collaboration with the banks, some building societies are now offering cheque book facilities and other banking services with accounts that pay interest. The minimum first payment is often quite high, and the interest rate low, and there may be other restrictions, but if you hate paying bank charges, these accounts are worth investigating.

Term shares
(capital bonds; high income shares/bonds)

Now that inflation has slowed down, and there is uncertainty about interest rates, these are less popular. In return for agreeing to leave your money with the society for a fixed period of time, you are promised a fixed interest rate, slightly higher than the going rate for Ordinary Shares. There is usually a minimum amount to invest, starting at £500.

Some societies will not allow money to be withdrawn early, unless you die, but most will permit you to take money out as long as you give the required period of notice, although there may be some loss of interest. You cannot add to a term share as you go along, apart from re-investing the interest, but you can buy new shares on the same terms if they are still available.

Extra interest accounts

These have taken the place of term shares at a time when interest rates are high, and expected to fall. Normally, you invest a minimum amount, which may vary between £500 and £10,000. In return for agreeing to give a fixed period of notice, usually one, two or three months, you receive a higher rate of interest, around 2-3 per cent more than for an ordinary account. Rates and conditions vary widely, so shop around.

In particular, read the small print to see what the rules about paying interest are. Some societies will continue to pay interest up to the date of withdrawal, others stop paying interest as soon as you give your statutory period of notice. And if you want to withdraw without the proper notice, you are likely to forfeit what you would have earned if you had given proper notice. So if you should have given three months' notice, you lose three months' interest, quite a substantial penalty.

Some societies will offer a dual account where you can withdraw without penalty at short notice, as long as you keep a minimum sum, which may be quite large, in the account.

Monthly interest

Many of the extra interest accounts and term shares will pay interest monthly. They may prefer to pay this into an ordinary share account, rather than sending it direct or paying to a bank. Monthly payments are worth more than the same rate paid annually, because you receive the money earlier and can re-invest it at once if you wish.

Special offers

Look out for these in the press, as sometimes a society will decide it needs a boost to its funds and launch an offer on exceptionally good terms. They may, for example, guarantee a good rate of interest for a fixed term. You have to be quick off the mark to take advantage of them, as if they are a bargain they are quickly over-subscribed.

Index-linking

The big criticism of building society investment was always that it did not keep pace with inflation, and the investment analysts take great delight in compiling charts to show just how much you would have lost if you had had your money in a building society over the last ten years. However, after the 1982 Budget became law, building societies were for the first time able to offer index-linked investments. The first to offer a scheme was the Alliance Building Society, who put out details of its scheme even before the 1982 Finance Act had made it legal. When it was launched, it sold out almost immediately. The scheme invited a minimum investment of £500, maximum £10,000, for a five-year term. Investors who leave their money in for five years get a 10 per cent bonus on the original amount at the end of the term, free of basic rate tax, while the investment will have been revalued month by month according to the Retail Prices Index.

The fall in inflation rates has made these schemes very much less popular, and there are very few on offer at the moment, though this may change if inflation is expected to rise sharply.

Points to watch

- When the building society says 'extra interest guaranteed' it is not guaranteeing the actual interest rate, only that it will be 1.5 or 2 per cent or whatever *above* the normal Ordinary Share rate. So if that falls, the extra interest rate will fall too.
- The building societies are not in the business of giving something for nothing, any more than any other commercial enterprise, so when they offer a higher than normal interest rate there is bound to be a catch in it somewhere. It could be a special opportunity worth seizing, but read the small print

carefully to see if there are hidden penalties, or if a long period of notice is required during which you get no interest.

- Some societies offer special terms to young savers, but there may be a limitation on withdrawals for people under the age of 18.
- Most term shares have some provision that the full interest rate is payable in the event of the holder dying before the term is up.
- Some societies, offer their own Granny Bonds for people over 60 or 65. These are subject to the same kind of rules as term shares, but may offer special concessions for joint accounts if one of the holders dies. They are not tax free, as the National Savings variety are, so would affect the calculations for higher rates of tax and age allowance.
- Small societies within the BSA often offer bargains if you are prepared to take the trouble to search them out, find a branch near you, or deal with them by post.

Summary

SAFETY

Will the capital be repaid in full?	Yes.
Are the investments officially regulated?	Yes.
Is the capital protected against inflation?	No, except index-linked schemes.
AVAILABILITY	Excellent.
METHOD	
How do you invest?	Through local branches or direct by post.
Are there commission charges?	No.
Are there extra charges when you buy and sell?	No.
INCOME	
Is income paid regularly?	Yes, half-yearly or some monthly.
Is it guaranteed?	No, depends on money market.

Are there prospects for capital gains?	No.
Is the income high/average/low?	Depends on scheme.
TAXATION	
Is the return assessed for income tax?	Yes.
Is basic rate deducted?	Yes.
Can the tax be reclaimed?	No.
Is it assessed for age income relief?	Yes.
Is it assessed for capital gains tax?	No.

Chapter 3

High Street Banks

This chapter is concerned with investment in the joint stock or clearing banks, the familiar banks on every street corner. You can also invest in fringe banks, foreign banks, offshore banks, and finance company banks, but that is not what we are concerned with here. However, we have included the National Girobank and the Trustee Savings Bank as they offer similar terms and facilities to the High Street banks.

Banks have the same advantage as the post office and the building societies, ubiquity. You have no problem in finding one if you want to invest. But some people seem to find banks more intimidating than the post office or the building society; witness the customers who prefer to queue outside the bank to use the cash dispenser rather than inside to see the cashier.

Somehow, a bank impinges on the traditional English reticence about money matters. There is the feeling that the girl behind the counter knows exactly what you are paying whom, and how near the bone your finances are: suppress these guilt feelings by reminding yourself that customers bringing in their money keep the banks in business, because banks do have some advantages.

The Big Five – Barclays, Lloyds, Midland, NatWest, Williams and Glyn's – between them control most of the banking business, and many apparently independent regional banks usually turn out to be subsidiaries of one or other of the big groups.

How safe is your money?

As far as the safety of your investment is concerned, you can be sure that if one of the big banking groups goes bust the country is in such trouble that no investment will be safe. In any case, the Deposit Protection Board guarantees that small investors (up to £10,000) will get 75 per cent of their money back if a recognised bank or licensed deposit taker gets into financial difficulties.

Is there any limit on investment?

Anyone can put their money in a bank, and there is no limit on the total amount you can invest, although there may be limits for special schemes.

How do you invest?
You simply choose your bank and the most convenient branch, and walk in; they will be glad to see you.

What return does it provide?
The big banks used to tie their lending rates to the Bank of England minimum lending rate (MLR) but as this has now been discontinued they have to fix their own base rates according to the money markets. Most other interest rates, to lenders and borrowers, relate to their *base rates*. Borrowers from the banks have to pay above base rate, lenders to the banks get less than base rate, unless they are exceptionally valuable customers. You'll find the base rates of the leading banks published regularly in the financial press.

Banks normally calculate interest on a day-to-day basis, so you get interest for every day that your money is in the bank. This is usually paid half-yearly. They may also offer special investment schemes with different arrangements for paying interest.

It's a sore point with many people that you don't get interest on current accounts, that is the ordinary bank accounts used for everyday money transactions, though it is not difficult to find a bank that gives you free banking if you remain in credit.

Most banks nowadays offer some kind of cheque-save account. These give you a cheque book, and pay interest on all or some of the balance remaining in the account. Some of these schemes are operated jointly with a building society.

The snags are that you may need a large deposit to open the account, and the amounts you have to keep in the account may also be substantial. There may be limits on the number of transactions per month, and you may not be able to withdraw cash as often as you like. Most people find that a cheque guarantee card is essential for paying by cheque, but some of the schemes do not provide them.

You would probably still need a current account or ordinary building society account as well as the cheque-save account, though it might save you some money.

All of which goes to show that you should keep the minimum necessary in your current bank account to avoid bank charges, and put the rest somewhere more profitable.

How is it taxed?

The 1984 Budget changed the rules about the way the banks paid interest on investments. Banks can no longer pay interest in full without deduction of tax. From the beginning of the tax year 1985-86 they pay a special composite rate, (see p. 158) like the building societies. Basic rate taxpayers have no more to pay, higher rate taxpayers may have to pay more, and non-taxpayers cannot reclaim any tax paid on their interest.

You have to include interest received from banks when adding up your income for higher rate tax and age allowance.

What types of investment are there?

The banking groups run all kinds of subsidiary companies, unit trusts, investment trusts, venture capital funds etc, and some of these are discussed later. The ordinary local branch of a High Street bank offers three main opportunities to investors:

Deposit accounts

Anyone, including children under 16, can open a deposit account with as little as £1 and no maximum whether or not they have a current account at that bank. Money can be paid in at any branch when it's open. If you have a current account as well, it's easy to transfer money between the two. The money can be withdrawn at seven days' notice, or sooner with loss of some interest. The big groups all tend to offer the same rate on deposit accounts, perhaps 3 per cent below the base rate, because the competition between them is so keen that they keep in step, not allowing one to steal a march on another. The rates are usually below the building society Ordinary Share rate, in some cases as much as 1½ per cent lower.

Interest is paid for each day the money remains in the account and is credited to the account twice yearly. It's a very simple and convenient way of saving, though not especially profitable, particularly if you need the money quickly.

Regular savings accounts
(bonus accounts)

Like the building societies, banks may be prepared to offer slightly better terms to people who are prepared to save regularly, although these schemes are less popular and less profitable than they used to be. You have to make regular payments for at least a year, with a minimum payment of around £10.

Interest is paid for each day the money remains in the account. The interest is credited to your account, or paid direct to you, twice yearly without tax being deducted.

During each year, or possibly half-year, you can normally take out some cash once, and miss one of the regular payments into the account if you can't afford it that month, without losing the extra interest. If you break the rules, you get the ordinary deposit rate instead of the extra interest. You may get a bonus at the end of a one- or two-year contract if you keep to all the rules.

Investment accounts
(money market accounts)

This is where the banks begin to compete with each other in offering more attractive terms to investors. Investment accounts are usually for fairly large sums and there may be a maximum amount that can be put into any one scheme. The main kinds on offer are:

Fixed term, fixed interest. In return for leaving your money with the bank for a fairly short fixed term, usually one, three or six months, you are guaranteed a fixed rate of interest for the whole period, which is paid to you in full at the end. There is usually a minimum of £5000 and a maximum of up to £30,000 for this kind of scheme, and it pays about 0.75-1 per cent under base rate.

Fixed notice, varied interest. You can deposit your money with the bank for longer periods, promising to give a fixed period of notice, in return for which you receive a rate of interest that varies according to the money markets, but is always at least 0.75-1 per cent above the ordinary deposit rate and about 2 per cent under base rate. This interest can be paid to you yearly or half-yearly, and most banks offer some kind of monthly interest scheme. Again there is usually a minimum investment, sometimes as low as £2000, and a maximum of between £20,000 and £30,000.

Fixed term, varied interest. If you agree to leave your money in the bank for a fixed term – one or more years – banks may offer a high rate of interest, often 2 per cent above the normal deposit rate, depending on the length of time your money is tied up. This rate varies according to the money markets, so it may go up or down during the period.

Large deposits

If you have a large sum to invest, at least £10,000, the banks are prepared to offer special rates, according to the period of notice you would want to give to have the money back. For example, you may have sold your house and be waiting to buy another. For money you want back at seven days' notice, they will normally require a minimum investment of £50,000. If you are able to give longer notice they may accept £10,000 upwards. The interest rate depends on the money market and the notice period, and is usually about 0.75 per cent below base rate. You can find out about these special arrangements from the securities counter at a large branch, or from your bank manager.

National Girobank

The National Girobank services have the big advantage that they are available in most post offices during normal business hours and on Saturday mornings. The National Giro provides free banking while you are in credit, and can be used as an ordinary cheque account with its own cheque guarantee card. It pays no interest on personal accounts, but you can open a deposit account which does pay interest, and amounts from this can be freely transferred into your personal account when you need to spend the money. Interest is calculated on a daily basis up to the eighth day before the money is withdrawn. The interest is credited to your account every six months.

Like other banks, the National Giro now has to deduct tax at the composite rate, which you cannot reclaim if you are a non-taxpayer. In April 1986, when the normal base rate was 10.5 per cent, the Giro interest rate was 4.75 per cent net.

Full details from the post office, or direct from the National Girobank Headquarters, Bootle, Merseyside GIR 0AA; tel: 051-928 8181.

Trustee Savings Bank

The TSB has over 2000 branches, and offers most of the services provided by the main clearing banks, including a cheque account and cheque cards. It is open office hours, Monday to Friday. Some branches now open on Saturday mornings.

It has a range of investment accounts, which pay interest net of composite rate tax like the main banks. The very basic service account offers instant withdrawals, direct debit and standing order facilities and pays a net interest rate of 2 per cent. Other longer notice accounts pay more competitive rates, and there are special rates for large sums and long-term deposits.

TSB offers a regular savings scheme, Moneybuild, which in return for regular payments over five years provides free life cover, priority for a TSB mortgage and 6½ per cent interest a year. Moneybuild 60 + is a similar scheme for over 60s, paying slightly more without the life cover.

You can get full information about TSB services from your nearest branch, or write to Customer Information Service, TSB England and Wales, PO Box 99, St Mary's Court, 100 Lower Thames Street, London EC3R 6AQ.

Points to watch

● Many banks offer gimmicks to attract young savers. But since most children do not pay tax, an investment paying interest in full is better for children's savings.
● Don't forget that, although the bank will normally pay interest calculated for each day the money is in the account, cheques paid into the account may have to be cleared before they are credited for interest (in case they bounce). This takes anything from one to four days, depending on where the cheque originated.
● It's no good keeping money in your deposit account and running an overdraft on your current account. You lose both ways. You pay tax on the deposit account interest, and you cannot (except in special cases or for business users) claim the interest you pay on your overdraft against your tax liability. The banks won't stop your overdraft as they make more from it than they have to pay you for your investment, so watch it.
● If you can plan in advance how long your money is to be invested, the bank is probably not the best place for it.

The Banking Ombudsman

Since 1 January 1986, customers who can't get satisfaction from their bank have been able to put their complaints to Ian Edwards-Jones QC, the new Banking Ombudsman. He adjudicates on disputes over personal banking services arising after that date. You can contact him through the Banking Information Service, 10 Lombard Street, London EC3V 9AR; tel: 01-626 8486.

Summary

SAFETY

Will the capital be repaid in full?	Yes.
Are the investments officially regulated?	Yes.
Is the capital protected against inflation?	No.

AVAILABILITY	Good.

METHOD

How do you invest?	Through local branches.
Are there commission charges?	No.
Are there extra charges when you buy and sell?	No.

INCOME

Is income paid regularly?	Yes.
Is it guaranteed?	No, depends on money market.
Are there prospects for capital gains?	No.
Is the income high/average/low?	Average/low.

TAXATION

Is the return assessed for income tax?	Yes.
Is basic rate deducted?	Yes.
Can the tax be reclaimed?	No.
Is it assessed for age income relief?	Yes.
Is it assessed for capital gains tax?	No.

Chapter 4

Gilt-edged Securities and Other Loans

When the government, some other public body or large institution, wants to raise money, it can invite the public to subscribe to a loan, the terms for which will be fixed in advance, so the interest rate is the same throughout the life of the loan, and it will be repayable on a fixed date. Units of stock in these loans are often bought and sold on the stock market which is what makes them attractive to investors. You are not lending the money once and for all until the repayment date; you can cash in your investment and get at least some of your money back by selling your units of stock through the Stock Exchange.

British government stocks
(gilt-edged securities, or gilts for short)

When the government decides to borrow money from the public rather than raise taxes, it issues a new government *stock* or loan. The reason for the nickname *gilts* is that the certificates issued for these stocks used to be edged in gold. Government stocks are considered to be very safe investments on the principle that, if the government can't pay its debts, who can? They are not only safe, but fairly predictable, because of their fixed interest rates and repayment dates. You know exactly what the stock is going to earn over a given period.

By varying the terms on which it is prepared to issue new stocks, the government can use gilts to influence the money market, though it cannot afford to be too out of line with other rates. When it issues a large new government stock, the interest rates and repayment dates are bound to have some effect on all other interest rates and stock market prices generally.

There are about a hundred British government stocks on the market, with new ones being added from time to time as the government needs more money and the old issues expire. Some of the names recall days long ago, when a few thousands in 2½ per cent Consols was a sizeable fortune; others, like War Loan, have a bad name because they never paid their original owners a fair return after the war. Nowadays, gilts are back in favour, especially since the index-linked stocks have been introduced.

How safe is your money?
It's difficult to imagine a situation in which any government reneged on its obligations as far as government stock is concerned. If it did happen, no investments would be safe. You are more likely to lose from inflation than from a bankrupt British government. In periods of high inflation the fact that the repayment values are fixed and the interest rates do not increase means that those who hold on to them can lose a lot of money in real terms. And if you want to sell, you may get less than you paid when you bought them.

Are there any limits on your investment?
Anyone can buy gilts, and there is no limit to the amount you can hold – you can buy as many as you are able to find for sale at the price you want to pay.

How do you invest?
The stocks are issued in units with a *face value* of £100. When the stock comes to the end of its life, £100 is the amount that will be repaid for each unit, and the face value of £100 is what the interest is calculated on. However, you do not necessarily have to pay £100 for a unit, even when they are first on offer.

When the government first puts out a new stock, it invites investors to tender. You will see advertisements in the press with a coupon for you to fill in, usually naming a minimum price. Forms are available from your bank or stockbroker. You have to decide what you think a fair price would be, considering the terms the government is offering, and you send in your offer. The government looks at all the offers received and fixes a price, taking into account how much it wants to sell of the stock and the state of the market. All those who tendered at or above the striking price are given an allocation of units at that price, even if they offered more. (Sometimes stock has to be rationed because of demand.)

Not all the stock in a new issue is normally sold off on the day of issue, and the government broker puts the rest on the market at his discretion, at a price that suits the government and market conditions. It is then known as a *tap stock*, because the government broker turns the tap on and off, regulating the supply.

Another development is the use of new government loan stocks by the government broker without the formality of a public prospectus and invitation to tender. This is known as a *taplet* or *tapette* in stock market slang.

However, this happens only once in a while; you can buy or sell gilts every day on the stock market or through the National Savings Stock Register, just like other stocks and shares.

The market price of a £100 unit is decided by three factors:

The interest rate. The name of the stock includes the rate of interest the government is willing to offer when the stock is issued and it varies quite widely, from 10 per cent Treasury Stock 2001 to 3 per cent Exchequer Stock 1986. This is known as the *coupon.*

The redemption date. This is the date on which the government has promised to repay the loan. The nearer you are to the redemption date the easier it is to know how much the stock is really worth. (A few stocks have no redemption date.)

The state of the economy. When interest rates in general rise, gilts become less popular, as people get a higher return on their money elsewhere. When they fall, the fixed interest rates of gilts are more attractive, so their price goes up. The prices are printed daily in the financial press. You can buy existing stock either, as described on pp. 20-21, through the National Savings Stock Register, or through a stockbroker (see p. 59 on how to find a stockbroker). You can deal with a stockbroker through your bank, solicitor or accountant if you prefer.

You will have to pay commission on your buying and selling. The Stock Exchange lays down minimum rates, and it is more expensive to deal in small amounts through a stockbroker than through the NSSR. The commission is higher, eg £1.80 for £250-worth of stock as compared with £1 on the NSSR, and there may also be a minimum charge. If you deal through a bank, solicitor or accountant, the commission may be slightly higher by a few pence in the pound. (See p. 60 for stockbrokers' fees.)

If you are buying through the NSSR you can either specify how much you want to spend or how many units or parts of a unit you want to buy. When buying through a stockbroker there is a third option: you can specify the price you want to pay for a unit. The prices quoted in the press are an average of what buyers and sellers get; buyers pay a little more, sellers get a little less. They may be expressed in either fractions or decimals, or both.

Example
You decide that Exchequer 10½ per cent 1986 are a bargain at a quoted price of £99.5 for a £100 unit, so you telephone your stockbroker and ask

him to buy you £1000-worth. The cost works out at £996.25 for 10 units at an offer price of £99.625, plus the stockbroker's commission of 0.625 per cent – £6.22.

Then you think that you will sell your 50 units of 13¼ per cent Exchequer Stock 1987 as the quoted price has reached £100.75, so you send off your form to the NSSR and the next day, when they get your letter, they sell them and you receive 50 × £100.625 (the bid price) = £5031.25 less commission of £21. Simple, isn't it?

What return does it provide?
The stockholder receives interest at the fixed rate twice a year, on the face value of the units held, but it is not quite as simple as that. You have to relate the interest you receive to the price you actually pay for the unit of £100. So if the interest rate is 4 per cent and you paid £31 for a unit, your true interest rate, known as *interest yield* is $4 \div 31 \times 100 = 12.9$ per cent.

As the date approaches when the interest, or *dividend*, is due, the price of the units on the market changes to take account of this. Usually, the owner of the unit gets the interest for the whole six months, even if the unit was bought half-way through that period. But about five weeks before the interest becomes due, the stock is declared *ex-dividend*. If you buy after that, the person who sold the unit gets the interest. There is yet another complication, because three weeks before a stock is declared ex-dividend (except for War Loan and stocks near their redemption date) you can choose whether to buy ex- or cum- (with) dividend. You have to pay more for cum-dividend stock.

Redemption yield also has to be taken into account. When the prices of stocks are given in the press the last column of figures is normally the *redemption yield*. This is a calculation of how much you will earn each year from a unit of stock if you buy at the current price, and keep it until it is repaid at the end of its life.

Example
Suppose that in 1982 you bought a unit of the Fund 6 per cent 1993 for £64⅛, which gives you an annual interest yield of 9.636 per cent when the half-yearly interest is re-invested. Over 11 years you receive £6 a year interest half-yearly and in 1993 you are repaid £100. The gross redemption yield figure assumes that you have re-invested your interest over the 11 years, and takes into account the profit you make of £35⅞ when the stock is repaid. For this fund the redemption yield is 12.284 per cent, quite a bit higher than the annual interest yield.

How is it taxed?
Interest from gilts is taxable, and if you buy stock through a stock-

broker, or direct from the Bank of England when it is first issued, tax at the basic rate is deducted from the interest before you receive it. If you buy your stock through the National Savings Stock Register the interest is paid to you *without* deduction of tax. You still have to pay the tax later on if your income is high enough to be taxable.

The interest from gilts is assessed for higher rates of tax and age allowance.

Previously, you had to keep government stocks for at least a year if you wanted to escape capital gains tax on profits from selling them. From 1 July 1986, all sales of gilts will be free of CGT, but this also means that you cannot set off any losses on the stock against other capital gains that might be subject to the tax.

What types of investment are there?

Gilts are classified into four groups: *longs, mediums, shorts* and *undated*, according, surprise surprise, to the date on which they are due to be repaid, though the groupings vary. In the tables published by *The Times* for example, are:

Short-dated stocks are those due for redemption in the next five years, so you have the advantage of knowing what the yield is likely to be over a reasonably short time, and are less likely to suffer from wide changes in the value because of changes in the money market.

Medium-dated stocks have redemption dates between five and ten years ahead.

Long-dated stock is due to be redeemed in more than 10 years' time. Here the risks are correspondingly higher.

Undated stock. These are stocks like the notorious War Loan where there is no date fixed for redemption and it is, in fact, unlikely that they will ever be repaid.

Sometimes a range of dates for redemption is given, so that the government can choose which date suits it best, in which case the stock is normally grouped according to its earliest date. The price may be lower because the repayment date isn't fixed.

Index-linked stocks. The government now issues index-linked stocks, which pay a low rate of interest as well as being covered for inflation. You can buy some of them through the National Savings Stock Register. Both the interest rate and the face value of the £100 units are index-linked. The index-linking is related to the Retail Prices Index and the base is taken as the RPI for the month seven months before the date of issue. So Treasury Index-linked 2 per cent 2000, which was issued in July 1981, has as its base the RPI in November 1980.

To find the present index-linked value of a £100 unit, you take the RPI for the month eight months before the current month – say it was 321. You divide this by the RPI for the base date eight months before the stock was issued – say 297. So the present value is $321 \div 297 \times 100 = £108$.

The 2 per cent interest rate would also have gone up to 2.16 per cent. Interest is paid on the *face value* of £100 per unit, not the index-linked value.

If you buy stock when it is first issued and keep it till the end of its life you get the full value of index-linking. When you buy from the stock market, the index-linked increase is taken into account in the price you have to pay, so this may reduce its value to you. By selling index-linked stock before the redemption date you may lose money, if there is not much demand for that stock at that time and the price is low.

Example
If you had paid £100 for a £100 unit of Treasury Index-linked 2 per cent 1996 when it was issued in March 1981, and sold it 18 months later when the price had dropped to £90½ you would have made a loss that was not in the least compensated for by the interest you had received, or any index-linking, and was not even tax deductible for capital gains tax.

Local authority loans

Just as the central government prefers to issue loans rather than raise taxes, so local government prefers to raise loans rather than put up the rates. You can either invest for fixed periods with any local authority looking for loans – it does not have to be your own – or you can buy and sell local authority investments through the Stock Exchange. Either way, interest rates and repayment dates are fixed.

How safe is your money?

These loans are still safe investments. Local authority borrowing is controlled by the government and it is unlikely that any local authority will be allowed to go bankrupt. Perhaps it is worth stating, in view of the various controversies about the legality of local authority spending, that there can be no question of any loans being declared void because of improper use of funds, as they are regulated and protected by law.

Are there any limitations on your investment?
Anyone can invest in local authority loans and there is no limit to the amount you can hold. There is a minimum investment amount in some schemes.

What types of investment are there?
Two kinds of bonds offered by local authorities make up most of their borrowing, though investors with large sums of money, above £25,000 or so, may be able to negotiate special terms.

Town hall bonds
(also called advertised or over-the-counter bonds)
These are fixed-term, fixed-interest rate investments. There is usually a minimum investment of £500-£1000, though some authorities will accept £250 upwards. You cannot have your money back before the term is up. For £2.50 you can get a full list of all the local authorities offering this kind of bond, with current interest rates and minimum sums, from the Chartered Institute of Public Finance and Accountancy (CIPFA), Sterling, 65 London Wall, London EC2M 5TU; tel 01-638 6361. You can telephone them Monday to Friday, 10 am until 2.30 pm, to find out the best offers at the moment.

To invest in a local authority loan all you have to do is to get an application form from the relevant town hall, fill it in and send it back with your cheque. There are no extra costs. But check the rates before you sign, as they may have changed overnight.

The interest rates are around 0.5-1 per cent above or below the banks' base rate, depending on the amount you want to invest, the state of the money market, and the length of time – anything from one to ten years – that you agree to invest your money. The interest rates are fixed for the whole life of the loan, so if rates generally are likely to come down, these loans can be a bargain.

Some authorities pay interest as a lump sum at the end of the term, in which case the rate should be about 0.25-0.5 per cent higher. Otherwise, interest is paid half-yearly.

Tax at the composite rate is deducted from the interest before you receive it. You cannot claim a refund from the Inland Revenue if you do not pay tax. The income is taken into account for higher rate tax and age income relief.

A few authorities will accept investments of this kind for less than one year, when they are known as *temporary loans*. For these, the interest is paid either monthly or at the end of the term. The CIPFA list gives the details.

The terms vary, anything from seven days' notice of withdrawal upwards, and the minimum sum to invest also varies from £500 upwards.

The tax position of these loans depends on the amount, and the length of time you deposit the money. If the sum is less than £50,000, or the time less than 28 days, the composite rate is charged and cannot be reclaimed. Larger deposits for longer amounts of time are not subject to the new system.

Negotiable bonds

These are investments that can be bought and sold on the stock market.

Yearling Bonds are issued to the financial institutions every Tuesday on behalf of some of the local authorities on the Bank of England's list. All the issues made on the same day are at the same rate of interest which is fixed for the one-year life of the bond, hence the name yearling. If interest rates generally go down during the year, the price of the bond on the Stock Exchange will rise, and vice versa, but bonds are repaid at their face value at the end of the year. The minimum amount to invest is £1000 and you can only invest in multiples, not fractions, of £1000.

The only way for an individual to buy and sell local authority Yearling Bonds is through a stockbroker – you can ask your bank, accountant, or solicitor to negotiate with a stockbroker for you if you prefer. You can't buy direct from the local authority or the Bank of England, even when the bonds are first issued.

The stockbroker will charge commission according to the Stock Exchange scales, about 0.5 per cent of the cost of a £1000 bond, less for larger amounts. The banks will charge their commission too if you ask them to deal for you. There may be a minimum commission charge of £5-£10. You cannot choose which local authority to invest in; you have to take what is available from a particular week's issue.

The interest rate is decided according to the market at the time of issue. If it seems likely that interest rates will fall during the year, this is taken into account when the authorities fix the rate. Interest is paid direct to you half-yearly. Tax at the basic rate is deducted from the interest before you receive it. You can claim a refund if you don't pay tax. The income is taken into account for higher rates of tax and age relief. Gains and losses made on Yearling Bonds are assessable for capital gains tax.

Local authority stocks (also known as *corporation stocks* or *corporation loans*) work in the same way as British government stocks, see pp. 43-8. They have fixed interest rates and fixed repayment dates, usually with a life of six years or more. You can buy and sell them on the Stock Exchange through a stockbroker, though not through the National Savings Stock Register. You can also apply for them direct from the local authority when they are first issued. Look out for advertisements in the press. Their value fluctuates according to the market.

Qualifying corporation stocks, like other qualifying corporate bonds, ie those quoted on the Stock Exchange or Unlisted Securities Market, are free of Capital Gains Tax from 1 July 1986.

Investors in Industry

Investors in Industry, often known as 3i for short, was formerly called Finance for Industry. Since the change which made all banks deduct composite tax from interest, 3i no longer offers an investment scheme suitable for small investors.

Finance house loans

Finance houses, which are financial institutions providing hire purchase facilities and other forms of credit to individuals and companies, offer good rates of return on loans. There are also other similar institutions licensed to accept deposits from the public which accept the same kind of loan, for example the Co-op Retail Services Ltd.

How safe is your money?

The companies must conform to the rules governing their licence to accept deposits. In any case, most of the well-known houses are subsidiaries of the big banking groups, so your money is reasonably safe. It is as well to stick to the established groups, most of whom would be members of the Finance Houses Association, who would give you a list of names and addresses.

Are there any limits on investment?

Anyone can invest in a finance house deposit scheme. There are usually minimum amounts from £100 to £5000. There may be a limit of £25,000 to £50,000 on investment in any one scheme, though no overall limit on the total amount invested in different schemes.

How do you invest?

Write to the relevant head office for an application form and details or call in at any branch of the institution that interests you.

What return does it provide?

These are normally fixed-term, fixed-rate deposits, so the rate of interest remains the same throughout the life of the loan. (A few variable interest rate schemes with a fixed withdrawal date are also offered.)

They normally pay about 0.75-1 per cent above base rate, depending on how long you leave your money invested. The interest is usually paid half-yearly direct to you.

How is it taxed?

Tax is deducted from the interest payments at the composite rate and these are liable for income tax at higher rates and age allowance.

What types of investment are there?

Most companies offer a choice of terms depending on how long you want to leave your money invested.

You cannot change your mind once the money is invested, or get it back before the end of the term. When the term is about up the company will normally offer you new terms to re-invest the sum.

Zero Bonds

These are a way of raising money by issuing bonds repayable at face value on a fixed date. No interest is paid but the bond is issued at a price much lower than the face value so that investors can make a capital gain when it is repaid. At present bonds are mostly of interest to pension funds and other large investors, but moves are afoot to make them more accessible to small investors.

Points to watch

Gilt-edged securities and other loans

- If you think that the rate of inflation is going to rise in the future, index-linked gilts are preferable to ordinary gilts.
- If you think inflation is going to fall, ordinary gilts may pay a higher return.
- If you are worried about how much your nest egg will be worth in the future, index-linked gilts are worth buying, provided you intend to hang on to them till they are due for repayment.
- If you want a good income and don't pay tax, but are not so worried about the value of your capital, a high coupon gilt pays well.
- You risk losing more capital if you buy long-dated stocks.
- If you hope to make capital gains rather than income, gilts have advantages as they are not assessable for capital gains tax at all from 1 July 1986.
- Stocks that are selling at a low price can produce good tax-free capital gains if you keep them until the repayment date.
- If you are prepared to tie your money up for a fixed period you can buy short- or medium-term gilts knowing exactly what the return is going to be in interest and capital (though not allowing for inflation).
- The National Savings Stock Register has the advantage of paying interest on gilts without deduction of tax, which means that even if you have to pay tax in the end, you have the use of the whole amount until then.

Local authority loans

- The interest rates on town hall loans vary quite a bit, so make sure you get the best terms.
- You cannot get your money back early if you invest in a Town Hall Bond. Some authorities won't even repay early if you die.
- The commission charged by stockbrokers tends to make it uneconomic to deal in small amounts of local authority stock.
- Local authority bonds offer a safe and predictable investment with a fairly high income, especially for non-taxpayers, but if you need the money at short notice you may not be able to get it, or you may have to sell at the wrong time and lose on the deal.

Finance house and other loans

The terms offered by different institutions vary quite considerably, so shop around. Rates change rapidly, so when interest rates are falling, try to invest your money as soon as you know what the current rate is, as it may change overnight. (If interest rates are rising, it may pay to wait a few days.)

The loans offer a good rate of return, especially for basic rate taxpayers, as long as you don't need the money back quickly.

Summary

Gilt-edged securities

SAFETY

Will the capital be repaid in full?	Yes, at the end of term, otherwise depends on market.
Are the investments officially regulated?	Yes.
Is the capital protected against inflation?	No. Depends on market.

AVAILABILITY	Good.

METHOD

How do you invest?	Through NSSR or stockbroker.
Are there commission charges?	Yes.
Are there extra charges when you buy and sell?	Spread between buying and selling price.

INCOME

Is income paid regularly?	Yes, half-yearly dividend.
Is it guaranteed?	Yes.
Are there prospects for capital gains?	Yes.
Is the income high/average/low?	Depends on type of stock.

TAXATION

Is the return assessed for income tax?	Yes.

Is basic rate deducted?	Yes, except NSSR purchases.
Can the tax be reclaimed?	Yes.
Is it assessed for age income relief?	Yes.
Is it assessed for capital gains tax?	No.

Other loans and loan stocks

SAFETY

Will the capital be repaid in full?	Yes, at end of term, otherwise depends on market.
Are the investments officially regulated?	Yes.
Is the capital protected against inflation?	No, depends on market.

| AVAILABILITY | Fair. |

METHOD

How do you invest?	Through stockbroker or local authority.
Are there commission charges?	Yes for stocks. No for direct loans.
Are there extra charges when you buy and sell?	Spread between buying and selling prices for stocks.

INCOME

Is income paid regularly?	Yes, yearly, or half-yearly.
Is it guaranteed?	Yes.
Are there prospects for capital gains?	Yes, for stocks.
Is the income high/average/low?	High.

TAXATION

Is the return assessed for income tax?	Yes.
Is basic rate deducted?	Yes.
Can the tax be reclaimed?	Depends.

Is it assessed for age income relief?

Yes.

Is it assessed for capital gains tax?

No, unless they are not 'qualifying' bonds.

Chapter 5

The Stock Market

When dealings in shares first began in London coffee houses, it was because the merchant adventurers needed long-term loans to finance their voyages. In return for putting up part of the cost of the voyage the seventeenth-century investors got a share in the profits (if any) when the ship came in. The principle is still the same; numbers of investors put up the money for large organisations – public and private – to carry on their work. A market developed in buying and selling the claims investors had on the organisations, so that investors could get their money back, at short notice, if necessary. The profits they make out of this buying and selling are often greater than from the original investments, and are what keep the stock market going, even in bad times.

Organisations raise money by selling *securities* – the general name for stocks and shares of all kinds. *Stocks* normally refer to securities which pay a fixed rate of interest, eg British government stocks or gilts, and *shares* to all the rest. When you buy a share you become a part-owner or *shareholder* of the company. *Stock* in the singular may also be used to refer to any transaction in stocks or shares, eg, 'I bought some stock in M & S yesterday.'

The Stock Exchange

There are plans to change the British Stock Exchange's unique *jobbing* system of buying and selling shares in the near future. At present, there are no individual members of the Exchange, only member firms who are either *brokers* or *jobbers*. Until the plan to merge some of their functions is in operation, brokers deal with the customers, those who want to buy or sell stock, while jobbers deal only with other members of Stock Exchange firms, both brokers and jobbers. All shares are bought or sold through jobbers. Brokers act for a client, and make their money by charging commission. Jobbers act for themselves and make money by buying cheap and selling dear, if they can. If jobbers misjudge the market, it's their own money they are losing, so they need to be shrewd judges of their own sector, which is why all jobbing firms specialise, dealing in a particular kind of share – property shares, mining companies, industrials etc.

The floor of the Stock Exchange is divided into pitches, each dealing with one of the sectors, so the brokers know where to find someone interested in a particular kind of share, and unless dealings in that share have been suspended the broker is sure of finding a market in that share with more than one jobber offering to buy or sell it. If you would like to see how it works in practice, it's well worth going along to the Visitors' Gallery, open Monday to Friday, 9.45 am to 2.30 pm, admission free. The entrance is at the corner of Threadneedle Street and Old Broad Street, London EC2. There are also exchanges in many provincial cities, but London is the largest and dominates the market.

How safe is your money?

The Stock Exchange has a fund which may compensate investors for fraud or failure by Stock Exchange members, but it cannot protect you against losing your money by investing in the wrong shares.

The Stock Exchange is a market whose prices depend not just on the supply and demand for various stocks and shares, but also on the *opinions* held by the buyers and sellers about those shares. These opinions are affected by all kinds of influences: company reports, the state of the economy, newspaper articles, comments by people supposed to be in the know, rumours about takeovers, international affairs, the weather. But it is such a large market that the most violent fluctuations tend to get evened out, because there are always people looking for a profit by buying or selling against the trend.

It's a skilled business making money out of the market, and the rewards are so great that the competition is very keen. However, it's up to you to tailor the risks you take to suit your pocket and your ambitions. A good stockbroker will be able to give you plenty of advice, as will the financial press.

Are there any limits on investment?

Anyone can invest in the stock market, and there is no limit to your holdings of shares and stock, but the commission and other charges make it uneconomic to play the market unless you have at least £5000-£7000 to play with. If not, and you still want to buy stocks and shares, you are better off with unit or investment trusts or investment in gilts through the National Savings Stock Register.

How do you invest?

First find your stockbroker. Your bank, accountant or solicitor may be able to introduce you to a suitable broker, or may act as your agent in dealing with one. Or you can write or telephone to the Information or Press Department at the Stock Exchange (London EC2N 1HP; tel: 01-588 2355) who will provide a short list of brokers who may be prepared to take on your business. Before you make your choice, talk to the brokers on the list and, if possible, go and see them, as it's very important to have a good relationship with your broker. Once you have a broker, you can phone in your orders and they will be acted upon immediately.

When he gets your order, the broker will go into the market and ask several jobbers what price they are quoting for that share. The jobber will give two prices, say, 106-108p. At that stage the jobber does not know whether the broker is buying or selling. The difference between these two prices is where the jobber makes his profit – the jobber's *turn*. He buys at the lower price and sells at the higher one.

The broker will then do a deal with the jobber who offers the best price. A simple note of the bargain is enough to ratify it, and it takes effect from that moment. The broker then sends you a *contract note* setting out the details – date, share price and the *consideration*, which is the price of the share times the number of shares bought or sold, the broker's commission to be charged, and the stamp duty payable, if any. It also tells you when you have to settle up; for gilts this is usually the next day, but for other securities it will normally be a week or two.

Dealings are carried out in a working period called the *account*, normally 10 working days. (So you will see in the press statements like 'The account opened well with a large number of dealings'.) The working period gives the jobber time to manipulate his deals so that his buying and selling match up, and also gives some credit to investors, who nevertheless have to pay in full on the *settlement day* named in the contract note. Later on you will receive the share certificates, the legal documents from the company in which you have bought shares, which register you as a shareholder, but your ownership dates from the moment your broker agrees verbally with the jobber, regardless of when the share certificates are issued. The Stock Exchange's Talisman computer system speeds up the formal process of issuing and recording share dealings for those shares registered with it.

Stockbrokers' fees

Most stockbrokers do not make a charge for advice and supervision of their customers' accounts; they make their living on the commission they get from buying and selling stocks and shares for their clients. The Stock Exchange at present lays down minimum scales of commission, but the new plans will end this, and allow stockbrokers to set their own rates. The present minima are:

1.65 per cent on transactions up to £7000;
0.65 per cent on transactions over £7000.

There may be a minimum charge, say £10 per dealing. Some firms charge more than the minimum. You have to pay VAT on top of this.

In addition, there is the government stamp duty to pay (see p. 166) when you buy ordinary shares, preference shares and convertible loan stocks, but not other loan stocks and debentures. There may be small fees, less than £1, for the contract note etc.

If you ask your bank, accountant or solicitor or other adviser to act for you in buying stocks and shares, they either share the commission with the broker, or will charge you a fee. In either case it will cost you a little more than dealing directly with a stockbroker.

What return does it provide?

It's easy to forget that you will receive a regular income from the stocks and shares you buy, because so much attention is concentrated on the capital gains people hope to make from Stock Exchange dealings. But all stocks and shares produce some kind of interest or dividend. The *dividend* is the amount that the company pays to its shareholders out of the year's profits. The company's directors may recommend an *interim dividend* part way through the year, but the *final dividend* has to be approved by the shareholders at the Annual General Meeting of the company. Near to the date when the dividend becomes due, shares are sold *ex-dividend* and marked 'ex-d' in the listed prices, because the price has fallen to take account of the fact that the person selling the shares will get the dividend, not the buyer. A few days before the share goes ex-dividend you may be able to choose whether to buy *cum-* (with) *dividend*, or ex-dividend.

In fact, it is the *yield* rather than the dividend that interests the serious investor, because the yield is the return you get on the price you have to pay for the share, not its nominal value. This is given in the daily press reports; for example, when Sainsbury's 100p shares cost 390p, and the dividend per share was 4.5p the true *yield* on your investment was 1.7 per cent.

When you are dealing with a stock that will be repaid at a fixed time, the *redemption yield* takes into account the amount of gain or loss you make when the capital is repaid, assuming that you have re-invested the interest you receive from the stock along the way. (See British government stocks pp. 43-8 for a full explanation.)

Another important test of a stock, which is connected with the earnings of that particular share, is the *price/earnings ratio*. The P/E ratio tells you the relationship between the current price of the share and the amount it earned at the last dividend payment – price divided by earnings: in other words, how dear (or cheap) the share is, judged on the basis of the dividend you get from it. So if a share was priced at 102.75 and the dividend was 4.6p the P/E ratio is 22, very high. A share priced at 53p, paying a dividend of 7.1p would have a P/E ratio of 7.4, rather low. A low P/E ratio, indicating a high yield, can be a sign that the share is cheap, or good value; a high P/E ratio may show that it is expensive, or poor value.

You don't have to work these figures out for yourself; they are given in the daily reports of the Stock Exchange dealings in the financial press.

How is it taxed?

Dividends are paid to you after deduction of tax at the basic rate. So is the interest on fixed stocks, unless you buy them through the National Savings Stock Register. You can claim a refund from the Inland Revenue if you don't pay tax. Both have to be declared for income tax and age allowance.

Capital gains is not chargeable on British government stocks or other 'qualifying' bonds. Any gains or losses you make in buying or selling stocks and shares above your annual allowance for CGT will not be assessable for this tax.

What types of investment are there?

There are over 7000 quoted securities on the Stock Exchange, and there is also a market in unlisted securities and options to buy shares. So the choice is wide. The financial press publishes daily lists of current prices and dealings in shares, conveniently classified into different categories. The list will be headed with details of the current account period. The details given for each stock and share in *The Times*, for example, are highest and lowest prices over the year, average price of the previous day's dealings, price movements up or down, gross dividend, yield and the P/E ratio.

1985 High	Low	Company	Price		Ch'ge	Gross Div pence	Yld %	P/E
445	380	Brown Shipley	410	●	..	13.2	3.2	17.7
548	453	Cater Allen	478	●	−5	41.3	8.6	11.6
41	23½	Cattles	37½		−½	2.3	6.2	12.6
50⅝	34 11/16	Chase Manhattan	£43 1/16	●	−⅛	364	8.5	..
42 13/16	27⅞	Citicorp	£31⅜	●	−¼	206	6.6	..
72	35	Clive	37	●	..	1.3	3.4	6.7
55	27	Com Bank Wales	53		−1	3.0	5.7	11.5
75⅞	42¾	Commerzbank	£72		−¼	6.0	0.1	..
195½	104⅞	Deutsche Bank	£180½		−3⅜	1200	6.6	..
179	74½	First Nat Finance	162		−1	..	..	11.4
372	284	Gerrard Nat	284	●	−3	18.9	6.6	16.5
80	55	Guinness Peat	78		−1	2.6	3.3	13.7
195	131	Hambros	198		..	9.6	5.1	15.7
27	12½	Do (50p)	£22		..	95.7	4.4	18.4
371	273	Hill Samuel	343	●	−3	17.0	5.0	9.0
99	61½	HK Shanghai	63½	●	−4	.. b	..	..
283	233	Joseph (Leopold)	278	●	..	16.1	5.8	14.5
188	146	King & Shaxson	152	●	−2	11.8	7.8	18.3
580	375	Kleinwort Benson	575		..	21.4b	3.7	10.6
514	346	Lloyds	484		−8	26.9	5.6	7.4
42	22	Manson	34		..	2.1	6.3	13.0
768	398	Mercury Secs	663		−5	22.9	3.4	10.3
462	322	Midland	444		−5	36.4	8.2	7.3

1985 High	Low	Company	Price		Ch'ge	Gross Div pence	Yld %	P/E
464	308	Bowthorpe	389	●	..	8.2	2.1	18.8
208	104½	Br Telecom 90p P	202		−4	9.3	4.6	13.3
97	70	Brown Boveri Kent	78	●	..	3.6	4.6	10.7
31	11½	Bulgin (AF) 'A'	12½		..	1.9	15.4	29.1
309	97	CASE	119	●	..	1.9	1.6	10.0
653	440	Cable & Wireless	613		−22	13.6	2.2	20.2
378	195	Cambridge Elec	250		..	10.2	4.1	11.6
180	138	CAP Gp	180		+7	..	..	..
53	26	Chloride	46		−1	..	..	10.8
226	129	Do 7½% CPF	211		−2	..	..	..
265	193	Comcap	220	●	..	1.7	0.8	17.1
278	200	Cray Elect	268		..	4.2	1.6	29.3
240	95	Crystalate	120		−3	5.6	4.7	7.3
85	61	Dale Elect	68		..	6.4	9.5	23.7
180	97	Dataserv	175	●	..	1.0	0.6	..
29	14	Dewhurst 'A'	24½	●	+½	1.2	4.9	11.1
290	245	Domino	280		+3	2.5	0.9	32.6
45	31	Dowding & Mills	45		..	2.0	4.4	14.3
208	134	Dubilier	180		−4	4.0	2.2	13.2
393	255	Electrocomponents	393	●	..	7.9	2.0	24.4
60	37	Electronic Mach	42		..	1.0b	2.4	29.6
55	39	Electronic Rentals	46		..	4.6b	10.0	18.1
263	156	Emess Lighting	252		..	7.9	3.1	26.5

There are two main categories of securities, *fixed interest*, and *equities*.

Fixed-interest stocks

With these, the interest rate is fixed for the life of the stock, the best example being British government stocks or gilts. Local authority loans, loans to other public boards eg Agricultural Marketing Board, and to foreign governments and institutions all fall into this group. (See pp. 43-56 for full details.) Companies can also issue *unsecured loan stock* and *debentures* which have an extra guarantee in that the debenture trustees can sell off some of the company assets to pay the interest due if necessary. If a company has to be wound up because of financial troubles, debenture holders and holders of unsecured loan stock have a *prior claim* on the company's assets, ie they are repaid before the ordinary shareholders.

Preference shares are shares with a fixed annual dividend, but if the company does not make enough profit during the year no dividend may be paid. Most preference shares are *cumulative* which means that if they don't pay the dividend one year, it is added on to the payment due next year.

Convertible loan stocks are loan stocks which can be converted into ordinary shares of the company at a later date.

Equities

These are ordinary shares that give the shareholders a stake in the company, and entitle them to a proportion of the assets, or equity, of the firm. Nowadays, the big institutions, such as insurance companies and pension funds, own a much larger proportion of shares than private shareholders and have a big influence on the market. The shareholders own the company and in theory elect the board of directors to run the business for them. The annual dividend comes out of the company profits. If there are no profits, no dividend is paid.

This is where the money is to be made, in picking the right share at the right stage of the market, to make a profit from selling it when the market goes up. It is also where most of the risks are.

New issues

When a well-known company goes public, or a nationalised industry goes private, which in both cases means becoming a listed company, this is always a source of great excitement on the stock market. Companies can only go public if they have a capital value of more than £500,000, intend to sell off at least 25 per cent of their shares to the public and can produce a good profit record for the last five years. In return for being listed on the Stock Exchange they must agree to all its conditions, which include giving full information about the company to the shareholders and following the rules of the Takeover Panel if any merger or takeover is planned. The company decides how much it hopes to raise and how many shares it wishes to sell. Each share must have a *nominal* value, often 25p, sometimes called the *par* value.

If the company had to be wound up and you had a £1 share nominal value out of a total share capital issued by the company of one million £1 shares, you would be entitled to a one-millionth share of the company's assets, after all prior claims had been met.

However, the company does not have to issue its shares at the nominal value, and in fact very rarely does so. When Habitat went public, for example, 10 million 10p shares were issued, but the minimum price for each share was 110p. These shares were worth 143p about a year later. So you can see that the people who own companies can make a lot of money out of a share issue, for themselves and for the company.

There are two ways of putting the shares on sale, through an *offer for sale* where the company sells shares to an issuing house or stockbroker who then issues them to the public, or through a prospectus when the company offers its shares direct to the public. Usually, as in the Habitat example, a minimum price is specified and you have to tender your offer for the shares at what you think is a good price. The company or issuing house will then decide what the *striking* price should be bearing in mind the offers it has received. Everyone who has offered at or above the striking price gets an allotment of shares at that price, either the full amount requested, or a proportion.

This is where the *stags* you read about in the press come in. A stag hopes to get an allotment of a new issue which is likely to be over-subscribed, at a good price, and then sell the shares at a profit as soon as dealing in them begins on the Stock Exchange.

There is the extra advantage that you do not have to pay commission and stamp duty when you buy a new issue, though they are charged when you sell. Small investors may be given priority when shares are being allocated, especially when the government

SOMETHING like £3 billion was being wagered on a spectacular success for the Laura Ashley flotation in the City today as investors jammed Barclays Bank in Farringdon Street with last-minute applications.

Among the scrum was one burly bank messenger with a single cheque from a speculator, who had applied for the whole of the £62 million issue. There could well have been others, with early estimates suggesting that every share available could be sold 50 times over.

The professional stags recognise they will be "out of the money" for six days—the allotment letters are unlikely to be posted until next Wednesday—but hope to get enough, and at a big premium, to justify the interest payments.

© *London Standard*

is selling off some nationalised industry, so it's worth a try. It's a gamble, but it can be profitable, though sometimes it goes wrong, and you can lose heavily if an issue which looks likely to be very popular suddenly gets bad news in the couple of weeks between the offer and the first day's trading.

New issues can also be *placed* privately by the issuing house if there is doubt about public interest in the shares.

Rights issue

When a company already listed on the Stock Exchange wants to raise more money, it does this through a rights issue, so-called because the existing shareholders must have the right to subscribe for the new shares in proportion to the number of the shares they already own. The price of the shares will be lower than the current price on the market, so existing shareholders have an advantage – they can buy at a discount. A rights issue can give you the right to buy one share for every one you already hold, or some other proportion. In November 1985, for example, Crown House offered a one for five issue at 130p when their shares had a market price of 163p. So existing shareholders stood to make a gain even if the price fell to allow for the extra new shares.

The shareholders can take up all or part of their option to buy, either for themselves or to re-sell on the market, or can refuse to take up any. Like other new issues, a rights issue will normally be *underwritten* so that it can't be a total failure. This means that the underwriters (a firm or firms of stockbrokers or the issuing house) agree, for a fee, to buy up any shares not sold to the public, and re-sell them later.

Capitalisation issue
(cap issue, free bonus or scrip issue)

A company may transfer money from its reserves by an adjustment of its accounts to issue new shares to its shareholders in proportion to their existing holdings. The value of the existing shares on the market will then fall in proportion unless the share is very popular.

If you had 100 25p shares, priced at 107p, and the company made a one-for-one scrip issue, you would hold 200 25p shares, but the price might have fallen to 53½p a share. So cap issues do not increase the *value* of your holding, except in the long term.

The Unlisted Securities Market (USM)

For those not content with the 7000 listed securities, there is also a market in shares in companies that have not quite made it to full Stock Exchange status or for one reason or another prefer to remain unlisted. The unlisted companies have to undertake to keep to most of the Stock Exchange requirements, though some of the rules are less stringent than for full listing. For example, companies do not have to produce a full report from an independent accountant.

You can deal in unlisted securities in just the same way as in ordinary shares, through your stockbroker. The share dealings are included in the daily lists of Stock Exchange dealings. USM shares are identified by a symbol (ringed in the figure below), to show you which is which.

1985 High	Low	Stock	Price	+ or −	Div Net	C'yr	Y'ld Gr's	P/E
52	7	+Entertain Prod 5p	10		b†2.25	2.1	32.1	1.8
82	50	Fairline Boats 10p	82	+1	†2.63	2.6	4.6	11.7
391	228	First Leisure £1	388	+4	†6.5	2.8	2.4	18.1
69	51	GRA Group 5p	67		—	—	—	8y.4
32	25	Grampian TVA 10p	28xd		†h1.67	♦	8.5	♦
35	10	+Greenwich Cable Comm	15		—	—	—	—
175	117	HTV Non/Vtg	175		7.7	2.9	6.3	7.8
148	78	Horizon	93	−1	♦4.4	3.6	6.8	4.2
140	95	Intnl Leisure 10p	102		4.8	3.1	6.7	5.6
252	100	Juliana's Hldgs 2p	100		†2.0	1.8	2.5	26.5
300	217	LWT	263xd		14.4	♦	7.6	♦
38	25	+Leisure Inv 10p	35		n—	—	—	♦
65	53	Leisuretime Int 10p	62		†2.1	3.9	4.8	6.6
115	98	+Lewmar	100		u2.63	3.0	3.7	12.4
183	153	+Media Tech Int 20p	167		g2.58	5.4	2.2	13.6
205	124	Medminster 10p	155xd		5.35	2.0	4.9	14.2
280	175	+Miss World 10p	180		3.6	4.1	2.9	12.3
127½	68	Nationwide Leisure	68		t3.75	2.5	7.9	6.0
39	11½	+Nimslo Int 20c	11½		—	—	—	—
27	19½	+Owners Abroad	22¾	+½	1.0	2.2	6.3	10.2
54	36	Photax (Lon.)	42	−4	—	—	—	—
241	10	+Philly Radio NV 5p	22½	+1½	1.8f	1.1	11.9	11.1

© *Financial Times*

There are certain tax advantages in dealing in the USM (see p. 137).

The trick seems to be to pick the right company very early on and sell out before the going gets rough.

A recent article in the *Financial Times*, on the USM's fifth birthday, suggests that the USM has been a 'bruising' place for the early investors. Lucy Kellaway estimated that £100 invested in the first 11 companies would now be worth £40, compared with £225 if the money had gone into the FT's top 30 companies. She concludes: 'The USM has provided small and immature companies with the chance to prove themselves and to blossom and grow if they can,... the great difficulty of sorting the winners from the losers has too often made the USM worrisome and unprofitable for its investors.'

The Over-the-Counter Market

You can also buy shares in companies not listed on the Stock

Exchange on the *over-the-counter* market. Licensed dealers offer shares for sale direct to the public in well-established companies that do not want a Stock Exchange listing, usually because they wish to maintain their independence. You may find that the dealer will vet prospective purchasers to make sure that they are 'sympathetic' to the needs of the company, (not making a disguised takeover, for example).

Over-the-counter dealers can advertise in the financial press, or you could get information about them from NASDIM, the National Association of Securities Dealers and Investment Managers, 28 Lovat Lane, London EC3R 8EB; tel: 01-283 4818.

Traded options

The traded option market allows you to increase or decrease the risk element in buying stocks and shares. You can either use it in a speculative way, in the hope of making gains, or to protect your existing investment by planning ahead. Instead of buying the actual stocks and shares, you buy an option on them which gives you a right to buy or sell shares at a specified price within a certain length of time. You can also buy index options which relate to the rise or fall in the FT-SE 100 Index (see p. 178).

The attraction is that you can back your hunches with a much smaller amount of capital than you would need to buy the actual shares – hundreds of pounds rather than thousands. It must be emphasised that, although the amount you are risking is less, there is still a considerable element of risk involved.

You deal with the option market through a stockbroker as for ordinary shares. You order either a *call option* in one of the shares, which means that you want an option to *buy* shares, or a *put option*, which means you want an option to *sell* shares. The *contract* you make will be for an option on 1000 shares and will specify the expiry date of the option and the price at which you can buy or sell the shares.

Each share has three classes of option each with a life of nine months, expiring at three-monthly intervals. As one class expires another is introduced. So in November 1985 you could buy options in Marks and Spencer expiring in January 1986, April 1986 and July 1986. The contract tells you the exact date in the month on which the series expires.

The *exercise price* – the price at which you have an option to buy or sell the shares – varies within the class, so you have not only a choice of dates but a series of share prices to choose from. Glaxo, for instance was offered at four share prices for each class in November 1985, when the current share price was 1560p, namely:

		Calls			*Puts*		
		Dec	May	June	Dec	May	June
Glaxo	1400	180	240	270	9	22	35
(*1560)	1450	130	200	235	15	25	45
	1500	85	165	200	25	40	65
	1550	55	135	165	45	70	85

So a Glaxo call option on 1000 shares in the December series at an exercise (share) price of 1500p would have cost you the hefty sum of £8500, plus commission etc, the price being so high because the time was nearly up. A put option to sell at the same price would have cost only £2500, for the same reason.

You can see that, although there are only a limited number of shares in the traded option market, there is plenty of variety.

The minimum amount you can buy is one whole contract for 1000 shares, and you may not hold more than 1000 option contracts for the same class of share. You can exercise your option to buy or sell at any time during its life, but you do not *have* to exercise it. You can sell the contract before the expiry date, or you can let it lapse.

All the transactions are monitored and registered by the London Options Clearing House, a subsidiary of the Stock Exchange. The brokers charge commission on option contracts, £1.50 per contract, plus a percentage of the option cost: 2.5 per cent on the first £5000; 1.5 per cent on the next £5000, and 1.5 per cent above that. There is usually a minimum charge of £10. You have to pay VAT on the total commission.

So if you bought 10 contracts of ICI at 6p per share this would cost:

10 × 6 × 1000		£600.00
Commission on contracts		
10 × £1.50	£15.00	
2.5 per cent × 600	15.00	
	£30.00	
VAT at 15 per cent	4.50	
Stamp duty	.30	
		£634.80

If you buy and sell at the same time, or within a short period, there is a reduction in commission costs.

There is a lot of skill and knowledge involved in playing this market, and plenty of scope. The price you pay for an option depends on how long it still has to run, the exercise price at which shares may be bought and sold, the state of the market generally, and how shares in that particular company are doing at the time. But you are risking much less than you would by buying shares and stand a chance of proportionately higher profits if you make the right decisions. The Stock Exchange produces some useful booklets about the Traded Options Market, available free from the Information Department (London EC2N 1HP).

Other share options

The options traded on the Stock Exchange should not be confused with other share option schemes. Traditional *stock options* are a direct bargain between two parties, arranged by a stockbroker, to buy or sell a fixed number of shares at a specific price within a certain time. These bargains can be arranged for most stocks and shares apart from gilts.

Many companies offer share option schemes to their employees which give them the right to buy the company's shares more cheaply than they would otherwise be able to do. There are some *savings related share option schemes* approved by the Inland Revenue where you save under an SAYE contract (see p. 99) and when you have completed the contract the proceeds are used to buy shares at a price fixed when you started saving, normally a little lower than the market price at that time. You can get all the details from your employer if this kind of scheme is available to you.

Personal Equity Plan scheme

In the 1986 Budget, the government announced the introduction of this scheme from 1 January 1987 to encourage individuals to save through purchasing shares. The investment funds will be paid to an authorised manager who will invest them in equities. The PEP manager will deal in shares on behalf of the investing individuals; the shares must be ordinary shares quoted on a UK Stock Exchange or dealt in on the Unlisted Securities Market.

The investing individuals must be UK residents and will be able to invest up to £2400 in a PEP each year. Proceeds from sales and dividends may be retained within the Plan and used to buy further shares over and above the £2400 limit.

Provided the investment is maintained for a minimum period (between 12 and 24 months, depending on when the Plan is started in the year) no tax will be payable either on the capital gains or on the re-invested dividend income.

Unit trusts

Unit trusts are a way of investing in the stock market indirectly; a kind of investment co-operative, as it were, where a number of investors put their money together so that the management of the trust can invest it for them in a range of stocks and shares. Each unit represents a share of all the amounts invested in different stocks and shares by that trust.

Investment trusts appear to do something very similar, but there are important differences between them: to invest in a unit trust, you buy units from the unit trust company and can sell them back only to the company. You can buy shares in an investment trust on the stock market, and you can sell the shares on the market too.

Unit trusts can invest only in stocks and shares quoted on the Stock Exchange (apart from a few unlisted securities). A recent change has allowed them to invest in other unit trusts, to create a 'fund of funds'. Investment trusts can invest freely in property and unquoted companies as well.

There is no limit to the size of a unit trust. This depends on how popular it is with the investing public; the more who subscribe, the bigger the trust gets. Investment trusts are limited in size to the amount of share capital laid down when the trust was formed. If more people want to subscribe to an investment trust, the price of the shares goes up, but the trust does not get larger.

How safe is your money?
Because unit trust companies are putting your money into stocks and shares, the value of the units goes up and down according to the stock market, and unit trust companies are obliged to include a 'government health warning' to this effect in their advertising. With this proviso, however, they are a safer way of investing in the

stock market than buying shares yourself as they can afford to spread their investments over a wide range of companies, which means that the risk is spread too.

Authorised unit trusts, ie those approved by the Department of Trade and Industry, must not invest more than 5 per cent of their money in any one firm, must not hold more than 10 per cent of the shares of one firm, and must not invest more than 5 per cent of their money in unlisted securities.

Unit trust companies are bound by the terms of their *trust deeds* which lay down the ground rules about the aims of the trust, how they are run, and the scale of charges they can make. They must have a *trustee* – usually one of the big banks or insurance companies – who supervises the operations of the unit trust company, and prevents fraud by holding all the assets in its own name, so none of the managers can embezzle them.

Offshore trusts, based in tax havens like the Isle of Man, are not subject to these disciplines. Small investors without special experience do well to be wary of unauthorised or offshore trusts, however good their performance appears to be.

Is there any limit on investment?

Anyone can buy units in a unit trust, and there is no limit to the amount you can hold. There may be a minimum investment of £500 or an equivalent number of units.

When buying units for children under 14 it is usual to have these put in a specially designated account, with one or both parents as nominee. From 14 to 18 the units may be registered in the child's own name, or still held by the parent as nominee. The nominee's consent would then be required before the units could be cashed in.

How do you invest?

The big advantage of unit trusts is that you can buy and sell units at any time. The unit trust company must always agree to sell or to buy back its units if asked to do so. You either buy direct from the unit trust company, or through an agent such as a bank, solicitor, accountant etc. You can telephone a trust direct and place your order, or ask for information and an application form. Unit trusts are heavily advertised in the financial press. You can write to the Unit Trust Association, Park House, 16 Finsbury Circus, London EC2M 7JP; tel: 01-628 0871, for a list of its members. The Association produces a very helpful leaflet *Explaining unit trusts* (free with sae) which includes suggestions about what you need to know about a particular trust before investing in it.

The price of the units in a trust varies according to the stock market value of the investments the trust holds, so it can rise and fall along with the market, or the particular segment of the market in which it specialises. Some trust managers will be more skilful than others in maintaining or increasing the value of their portfolios (which is why you should look at performance tables before choosing a trust). As with stocks and shares there are in fact two prices, a buying price and a selling price.

You buy at the *offer* price and sell at the *bid* price, about 3.7 per cent lower. The difference between the two is called the *spread*. There are also charges: an initial fee to cover stamp duty, Stock Exchange fees and other expenses when you buy the units, which is incorporated in the spread and forms part of the offer price, and an annual management fee, about 0.5 per cent of the value of the units, plus VAT. If you buy through an agent he will charge his commission too. The charges work out less than small investors would have to pay if they dealt direct with the stock market.

The financial press gives regular information about the performance, price, and dealings in unit trusts. For example, *The Times* publishes a daily table listing all authorised unit trusts in alphabetical order of their managing groups. The table gives the current bid and offer prices, changes during the week, and the yield.

	Bid	Offer	Wkly Chng	Yld
GOVETT (JOHN) UNIT MANAGEMENT				
Winchester Hse, 77, London Wall, London EC2N 1DA				
01-588 5620				
Intl Growth	61.6	65.8	+0.2	1.81
American Growth	51.2	54.7	+1.3	0.32
American Inc	60.0	64.1	+1.4	5.02
European Growth	133.3	142.5●	-1.8	0.31
Gold & Minerals	42.8	45.7	+0.2	1.86
Japan Growth	90.4	96.6	-1.3	..
Pacific Income	60.1	64.2	-0.7	4.22
UK Special Opps	71.0	75.9	+0.5	2.39
GRE UNIT MANAGERS				
Royal Exchange, EC3P 3DN				
01-638 2020				
Gilt & Fixed Int	112.6	117.0	-0.3	9.70
Growth Equity	168.7	179.5●	-2.2	2.43
Guardhill	245.8	254.7	-2.5	3.34
N American	119.9	127.6●	+2.5	1.77
Pacific	140.3	149.3●	-3.2	0.58
Property Share	191.6	203.9	+0.1	1.95
Smaller Companies	168.8	179.6●	+0.6	2.07
European Trust	151.9	161.6	-2.2	0.73
GUINNESS MAHON UNIT TRUST MANAGERS				
PO Box 442, 32 St Mary-at-Hill London EC3P 3AJ				
Energy Intl	47.1	50.3	..	3.36
Do Accum	51.3	54.8	..	3.36
Extra Income	126.4	135.1●	-1.9	6.16
Do Accum	223.3	238.8●	+1.6	6.16
German Gth	46.4	49.6	-2.3	0.54
Do Accum	46.4	49.6	-2.3	0.54
Income	227.4	243.2●	+1.5	4.78
Do Accum	441.1	471.7●	+3.8	4.78
Intl Tech	146.1	156.2●	-0.3	0.74
Do Accum	152.4	162.9●	-0.4	0.74
N Amer & Gen	86.2	92.1	+2.0	1.43
Do Accum	92.2	98.6	+2.2	1.43
Pacific Basin	86.3	92.2	-1.4	0.59
Do Accum	89.4	95.6	-1.4	0.59
Smaller Cos & Rec	148.3	158.6●	+0.2	2.13
Do Accum	165.2	176.6●	+0.2	2.13
Worldwide Growth	144.5	154.5	-0.1	1.35
Do Accum	201.3	215.2	-0.3	1.35
LLOYDS LIFE UNIT TRUST				
20, Clifton St, London EC2A844X				
01-920 0311				
Equity Dist	91.2	97.1	+0.3	1.64
Do Accum	126.5	134.6	+0.4	1.64
Gilt Trust	49.3	51.9	-0.2	4.81

© *Times Newspapers Ltd*

What return does it provide?
In the unit trust world, the interest you receive is known as the

distribution; the money the unit trust's investments have earned, less the management's expenses, is *distributed* to the unit holders. You will either receive this direct from the company, normally twice a year (more frequently for some high income trusts) or you can leave it in the trust to *accumulate* and build up the size of your investment. You may be able to choose to take some income out and re-invest the rest. Most companies offer a choice of distribution or accumulation units in the same trust.

Another option is a trust which agrees to pay out a fixed income which is made up from distribution payments, plus withdrawals of capital from the units as they increase in value. Of course, if you do this when the units are *not* increasing in value, you are using up your original capital and may get less back in the end than you began with.

To work out what rate of return you are receiving, or the *yield* of your units, you divide the distribution you receive during the year by the price you paid for your unit, and turn it into a percentage. So if you paid 40p for a unit, and received 2p distribution, the sum would be $2 \div 40 \times 100 = 5$ per cent.

As the time for paying out the distribution draws near, the price of the units rises to take account of the amount that will be paid out. When the units are marked ex-distribution (xd) the seller gets the distribution due, not the buyer, and the price then falls to take account of this change.

How is it taxed?
Unit trusts themselves have a big advantage as the gains they make on their investments are not subject to capital gains tax. That means they have more to distribute to their holders. But any gains you personally make on your holding are subject to capital gains tax if they take you over your £6300 minimum. Tax on unit trust distribution is on a current-year basis, so you pay the tax in the year you get the income. The distributions of income from the trust are taxed at the basic rate before you get them; you can claim a refund from the Inland Revenue if you are a non-taxpayer. You will be subject to higher rates of tax if your income is high enough and the amounts are taken into account for investment income surcharge and age income relief.

If you leave your money in the trust to be re-invested, the same rules apply; you don't escape the income tax. The trust should send you an annual income statement for any accumulation units you hold.

What types of investment are there?

Whatever your needs or interests, you should be able to find a unit trust to suit you. There are about 700 authorised trusts currently on the market, a bewildering variety to choose from. You can classify them in two ways – according to their financial aims, and according to the sector they invest in. Financially, there are three main options: income, capital growth, or a mixture of the two.

High income trusts concentrate on buying shares in companies that are likely to give a high yield to distribute to holders. They would be advertised as aiming to provide a yield as much as 50-60 per cent above the FT All-Share Index.

'High yielding shares are traditionally associated with above average risk, but the diversity provided by a well-spread and actively managed portfolio means that this risk can be greatly minimised', as one advertisement puts it.

Capital growth funds, or performance funds, hope to increase the capital value of the investment portfolio. A typical description would read, 'Entering these more adventurous areas means higher growth potential, but unit prices could have more marked and quite frequent fluctuations.'

General or mixed funds aim to produce both capital and income and a recent development, sometimes called a rainbow fund, allows the investor to select what proportion of his or her savings should go into the different funds, colour-coded by their type (hence 'rainbow').

All trusts reflect the behaviour of the stock market, and just as certain kinds of share are more prone to violent fluctuations in value, so unit trusts specialising in that kind of share cannot escape some of these ups and downs. *Recovery trusts*, for example, specialise in buying up shares in companies that have done badly in the recession, but look as though they may revive. This is a high risk area, as the trick is to buy the shares before anyone else notices that they may be a bargain, while at the same time avoiding those that will never be a bargain again. *Overseas trusts* concentrate on investment in foreign companies, often specialising in particular areas. (NB. These are not *offshore funds*; they are authorised British unit trusts which buy foreign shares quoted on stock exchanges.) There are *gilt and fixed interest trusts*, or you can even buy units in a unit trust concerned with investment trust companies and get a double spread of investment.

Commodity trusts, specialising in gold, oil, energy, mining etc are also very vulnerable to fluctuations, because the price of commodities tends to rise and fall with great rapidity. In recent years, it has fallen more often than risen. They are a very speculative investment. Several trusts nowadays cater for *charities* and special causes such as Mencap.

If the responsibility of choosing among all these is too much for you, there are management services who will manage your investment for you. They will select a portfolio of unit trusts and keep an eye on them for you, and will offer you a choice of strategies to meet your needs for income or capital. Although most require a large minimum investment, some cater for small investors. Charges vary, but should not be too high because the managers will be able to get commission from the unit trusts.

Many trusts put out free booklets describing their own products. If you want more detailed information, the Unit Trust Association publishes jointly with the *Financial Times* the *Unit Trust Yearbook*, which gives you all the data you could possibly need. It costs £12.50, but you should find it in a good business library.

Savings plans

If you cannot or do not wish to invest a lump sum in a unit trust, many of the unit trust groups offer savings plans, where you contribute a regular amount to whichever trust you choose. The minimum payment is usually £20 per month, or quarter; some trusts will accept any amount over £10 as and when you can afford it. The distribution on the units is re-invested and you receive an annual or half-yearly statement of the value of your accumulated investment. There may be a bonus for large amounts; for example in November 1985 the Framlington unit trusts would give you a monthly bonus of extra units equal to 1 per cent of your payment if you committed yourself to paying in £100 a month or more. You can withdraw all or some of the money at any time without penalty.

Savings plans are a way of avoiding some of the risk that a fall in stock market prices will wipe out the value of your units. The ups and downs of the market will affect the price of units each month, so in a bad month for the market you get more units, and vice versa. You don't have to worry so much about the timing of buying and selling units, as your investment over the year will automatically compensate to some extent for the market changes. (It won't help if the market collapses altogether.)

Share exchange plans

If you already own shares quoted on the Stock Exchange and would like to swop these for investment in a unit trust, many of the trusts are prepared to accept your shares either for their portfolio, or to re-sell for you. This may be a better bargain than selling the shares yourself and buying units with the proceeds, as you should save on commission and other costs. But check the small print, as some share exchange schemes are more generous than others.

Switching

Most unit trust managements offer several different kinds of trust and it is easy to switch your units from one trust to another under the same management. So if you are not satisfied with the performance of one trust, or think that another is likely to do better in future, you can change to another trust from the same stable at less than it would cost you to sell up and buy into a new group. Don't forget, however, the spread between the bid and offer prices of units. This still usually applies, though not always; you should get some kind of discount on the offer price if you are buying back into the same management.

Investment trusts

Like unit trusts, investment trusts spread the risks and the opportunities of playing the stock markets by investing in stocks and shares in a range of different companies. However, when you put your money into an investment trust you buy shares in a company that is itself listed on the Stock Exchange, where its shares are bought and sold. This is different from buying units in a unit trust, which are bought and sold only by the unit trust company. The value of your investment in an investment trust depends on the market price of the shares in that investment trust company and not, directly, on the value of the investments it holds.

Investment trusts can invest in things as well as in the shares of other companies, for example property such as office blocks; and they can buy shares in companies not listed on the Stock Exchange or on the Unlisted Securities Market. They can also borrow money to buy assets if they think this will be profitable.

One difference between them and unit trusts is that they are not allowed to advertise, except when launching a new issue of their own shares. This may be why they have not, in the past, attracted as much attention and money from investors as the unit trusts.

How safe is your money?

In order to be approved under the Finance Acts and so get tax concessions, investment trusts must be based in the UK, listed on the Stock Exchange, and get most of their income from stocks and shares. If they make capital gains on their investments, they must re-invest these in the business; they may not distribute this money to shareholders. They must not have more than 15 per cent of their assets in any one company. As public companies, they are regulated by company law; they also have to keep to the Stock Exchange rules for listed companies (see p. 63).

There are additional rules for companies who wish to become members of the Association of Investment Trust Companies. The Association does not regulate the affairs of investment trusts, but its standards of entry give some protection to investors. To be a member, an investment trust must hold at least 60 per cent of its assets in stocks and shares quoted on the Stock Exchange, which puts some limit on the number of high risk investments held.

The Association does not recommend individual trusts to investors, but it can give general advice and information; it publishes a useful guide *How to make IT: Your guide to investment trusts*, price £5.95, available from the Association at Park House, 16 Finsbury Circus, London EC2M 7JJ; tel: 01-588 5347.

If you put your money into investment trusts you must expect to see the value of your investment go up and down with the stock market. The prices that the market puts on investment trust company shares depend on the value of the trust's investments and also on the opinion the market has of how the company is being managed and the amount of borrowing it has undertaken.

Because investment trusts can borrow money to buy investments, this *gearing* (see p. 185) means that if prices rise, the ordinary shareholders of the trust will benefit more than they would have done if the trust had had to rely only on its own resources to buy shares and other investments. While prices increase, the value of the fund's portfolio will rise more quickly, even taking into account the need to repay the loans. But if prices fall, the trust may be left with heavy liabilities in the form of fixed interest loans with the result that there is less for the ordinary shareholders. So the prices of shares in investment trusts with high gearing may fluctuate more than the market as a whole.

Another factor that affects the value of your investment in an investment trust is the *net asset value* (NAV). The net asset value is the market value of the investments the trust owns after any borrowing has been deducted. It changes from day to day as the stock market prices move. The stock market price of shares in investment trusts is almost always *below* the net asset value of the investments the trust holds. This means that you are buying at an *asset discount* – you are paying less for the assets than you would have to pay on the open market. (If the share price is *above* the net asset value, the shares are said to be at an *asset premium*.) For example, if a share in an investment trust is priced at 143p, and the net asset value per share is 183p, you are buying assets at a discount of 40p which equals 22 per cent.

Of course, you may have to *sell* at a discount too, when you want to cash in your investment.

Is there any limit on investment?
Anyone can buy shares in investment trusts, and you can buy as many shares as you want. It's probably not worth investing less than £700 because of stockbrokers' charges.

How do you invest?
You buy and sell shares in an investment trust in the same way as any other shares, through a stockbroker, or through the stock-broker for your bank, solicitor, accountant etc.

The Association of Investment Trusts can give you a helpful list of stockbrokers willing to take on new investment trust business; it also gives the minimum investment they will handle. The stockbroker charges the usual commission on your dealings (see p. 60) and you have to pay stamp duty when you buy shares. There is no other charge when you buy or sell the shares, but annual management charges are deducted by the trust from the profits – at a fairly low rate, about one-third of 1 per cent of the net assets.

Investment trusts are listed in the financial press daily share tables. The table gives the year's highest and lowest prices, the current price, changes up or down, the net dividend, the dividend cover, and the gross yield.

The AITC publishes a guide for the private investor, *How to make IT*, costing £5.95. The annual *Investment Trust Yearbook* is more expensive, £50. The stockbroking firm of Wood Mackenzie, who specialise in investment trusts, publish regular reports and a

TRUSTS, FINANCE, LAND

1985 High	Low	Stock	Price	+ or -	Div Net	Cvr	Y'ld Gr's
		Investment Trusts					
101	87	Ailsa Inv.	98	.....	1.8	1.4	2.6
691	583	Alliance Trust	657	−3	†17.25	1.0	3.8
67	57	Altifund Inc..................	62	....	8.6	1.0	19.8
550	445	Do. Capital.................	550	....	0.43	1.0	0.1
245	183	Alva Investment Trust..	197xd	−1	‡2.9	1.0	‡
70½	61	Ambrose Inv. Inc.	63	.....	8.82	1.0	20.0
282	220	Do. Cap.	277	−5	—	—	—
154	118	American Trust	133	.....	†2.9	1.4	3.1
152	114	American Tst. '8'	130	.....	—	—	—
302	245	Anglo Am. Secs...........	282	.....	5.7	1.0	2.9
120	104	Archimedes inc.	120	.....	†9.0	1.0	10.7
125	92	Do. Cap. 50p.............	124	+1	..	—	—

© *Financial Times*

definitive annual guide with much analysis and information, but this costs even more – £250 a copy. You might be able to find one or other of these in a good business library.

So there is plenty of information available to help you find a trust that suits you.

What return does it provide?

The interest that the trusts receive from investments is distributed to shareholders after expenses and loan payments have been deducted. Approved investment trusts may not distribute any capital gains; these are all invested in the trust, and increase the value of the shares. Most trusts pay two dividends a year, an interim and a final dividend. These will depend on the performance of the companies in which the trust holds shares, and on the kind of investments it holds.

The *dividend* is the amount you receive per share; the *yield* is the rate of return on the amount you paid for the share, and this generally is given in the published share prices. Yields vary widely, the average being about 5-6 per cent. The price of a share in an investment trust company can change rapidly when the dividend day approaches, so you need to keep an eye on this and make sure you know when it's due. Many trusts are designed to produce capital growth rather than income, or a mixture of the two, so this brings down the average yield.

Don't forget to let the investment trust company know if you change your address. Like many similar organisations, it holds thousands of pounds' worth of unclaimed dividends whose owners it has not traced.

How is it taxed?
The income from investment trusts is taxed at the basic rate by the company before it is passed on to you. You can reclaim this from the Inland Revenue if you are a non-taxpayer. It must be declared for higher rates of tax and age income relief.

You have to pay capital gains tax in the normal way if your total net gains from investments are above the annual limit. But the investment trust companies have recently been exempted from paying capital gains tax on the gains and losses *they* make from buying and selling investments, and this has improved their profitability considerably in the last few years.

What types of investment are there?
Investment trusts specialise in much the same way as unit trusts. Some aim to produce high dividends or high capital growth, and others a combination of the two. The more different kinds of share in the trust's portfolio, the more likely the trust is to retain its value – safer, but perhaps not spectacularly profitable in good times.

Trusts may invest in a large number of different companies or perhaps just a few; some may back smaller companies and un-quoted securities; others may specialise in different parts of the world, in particular kinds of share, in oil or commodities, in gilt-edged securities, or in many other fields.

One point to be clear about is that the name of a trust may give little or sometimes the wrong idea about the kind of investment which is its speciality. Investment trusts have been going for a long time. Over the years the investment policy may have developed in a new direction, but the company does not want to change a well-known and trusted name. So don't take it for granted that a trust called the International Caledonian invests only in Scottish companies operating abroad. Maybe that's what it was launched to do in 1900, but times have changed, and policies with them.

Split-level trusts are those where the shares are split into two classes: one class provides income for the shareholders; the other promises capital growth. The date when the trust is to be wound up is normally fixed in advance. Until then, the income shareholders get most of the interest and dividends earned by the trust's investments and the capital shareholders get little or no dividend. When the trust is wound up, the income shareholders get back an amount agreed when the trust was launched; the capital share-holders are entitled to all the rest of the assets, ie they benefit from any growth in the value of the investments the trust has made. It is an expert task to decide whether or not a split-level trust is a good investment.

The Stock Exchange: Points to watch

- It would take more than this guide to tell you how to play the stock market. You need to make a study and a hobby of the market to have any chance of success.
- Remember that the *Financial Times* has a round-up on Saturdays of all the week's financial news and movements in Stock Exchange prices throughout the week.
- Your stockbroker will often be a good source of advice and help, but remember that he is not liable for any losses you may make through following his advice unless you can prove professional negligence.
- It could be negligence if, for example, you gave instructions to buy or sell and he delayed carrying them out so that you lost money.
- It's not negligence if you follow his advice and lose money, as long as the advice was reasonable in the circumstances.
- A stockbroker is not *obliged* to warn you that you are making a mistake; he has to carry out your instructions, and it's your responsibility if you ask him to do something foolish.
- Don't neglect the put (selling) options in the traded option market, especially if prices look likely to fall. If you have a guarantee of being able to sell at a fixed price, which might be higher than the market price, you can make a profit even out of a falling market.
- You don't *have* to gamble; there's nothing to stop you buying a few good stocks and shares, and keeping them as a long-term investment. You could even beat the speculators that way in the long run.

Stocks and shares: Summary

SAFETY
Will the capital be repaid in full?   Not necessarily; depends on the market.

Are the investments officially regulated?	Yes.
Is the capital protected against inflation?	Depends on market.
AVAILABILITY	Fair.

METHOD

How do you invest?	Through stockbroker.
Are there commission charges?	Yes.
Are there extra charges when you buy and sell?	Yes, spread between bid and offer price.

INCOME

Is income paid regularly?	Annual dividend.
Is it guaranteed?	No, except loan stocks.
Are there prospects for capital gains?	Yes.
Is the income high/average/low?	Depends.

TAXATION

Is the return assessed for income tax?	Yes.
Is basic rate deducted?	Yes.
Can the tax be reclaimed?	Yes.
Is it assessed for age income relief?	Yes.
Is it assessed for capital gains tax?	Yes (except qualifying loan stocks).

Traded options: Summary

SAFETY

Will the capital be repaid in full?	Not necessarily.
Are the investments officially regulated?	Yes.
Is the capital protected against inflation?	Not relevant.
AVAILABILITY	Fair.

METHOD
How do you invest?	Through stockbroker.
Are there commission charges?	Yes.
Are there extra charges when you buy and sell?	No.

INCOME
Is income paid regularly?	No.
Is it guaranteed?	No.
Are there prospects for capital gains?	Yes.
Is the income high/average/low?	Depends.

TAXATION
Is the return assessed for income tax?	No.
Is basic rate deducted?	—
Can the tax be reclaimed?	—
Is it assessed for age income relief?	No.
Is it assessed for capital gains tax?	Yes.

Unlisted Securities and Over-the-Counter Markets: Summary

SAFETY
Will the capital be repaid in full?	Depends on market prices.
Are the investments officially regulated?	Yes.
Is the capital protected against inflation?	No, depends on market.

AVAILABILITY	Fair.

METHOD
How do you invest?	USM: through stockbroker. OTCM: OTCM dealers.
Are there commission charges?	Yes.

Are there extra charges when you buy and sell?	Spread between bid and offer prices.

INCOME

Is income paid regularly?	Yes, annual dividend.
Is it guaranteed?	No.
Are there prospects for capital gains?	Yes.
Is the income high/average/low?	Depends.

TAXATION

Is the return assessed for income tax?	Yes.
Is basic rate deducted?	Yes.
Can the tax be reclaimed?	Yes.
Is it assessed for age income relief?	Yes.
Is it assessed for capital gains tax?	Yes (except for qualifying loan stocks).

Unit trusts: Points to watch

- It's a good idea to keep an eye on the *Financial Times* share indices to see that your chosen trust is keeping up with general performance of shares, or shares in its group.
- There's no shortage of advice about unit trusts, but you have to learn to judge the value of it for yourself, as for any other tipster.
- Unit trust managements with a good track record are likely to be more consistent in their performance than some of the others. The same names seem to crop up all the time in the performance tables so beloved of financial analysts. Magazines like *Planned Savings* and *Money Observer* will give you plenty of factual information about the performance of unit trusts. But don't forget that this relates to the past, not the future.
- Unit trusts may change hands, or be taken over, so make sure that the winning team you are hoping to back is still playing for the same company.
- If you are not satisfied, it's easy enough to cash in your units to start again, but don't do this too often, or any gains will be outweighed by extra costs.

- Though some trusts, eg the recovery trusts, are designed to make short-term profits, you should regard unit trusts as a long-term investment. You can lose a lot by having to sell out when the going gets tough, but if you are clever enough to sell out before then, so much the better. Timing is very important.
- Unit trusts have been criticised for advertising to attract unwary investors when the market is very high, without warning them that the higher it is the more likely it is to go down rather than up.
- Unit trust savings plans are usually better value than life-insurance linked plans (see p. 88) now that tax relief on life insurance premiums is no longer available.

Unit trusts: Summary

SAFETY

Will the capital be repaid in full?	Depends on market price of units.
Are the investments officially regulated?	Yes.
Is the capital protected against inflation?	Depends on market.

AVAILABILITY	Good.

METHOD

How do you invest?	Application to unit trust or licensed dealer.
Are there commission charges?	Yes.
Are there extra charges when you buy and sell?	Spread between bid and offer price.

INCOME

Is income paid regularly?	Yes.
Is it guaranteed?	No.
Are there prospects for capital gains?	Yes.
Is the income high/average/low?	Depends on type of trust.

TAXATION

Is the return assessed for income tax?	Yes.

Is basic rate deducted?	Yes.
Can the tax be reclaimed?	Yes.
Is it assessed for age income relief?	Yes.
Is it assessed for capital gains tax?	Yes.

Investment trusts: Points to watch

- Investment trusts have been unpopular in the recent past, and much of their thunder has been stolen by the unit trusts. But recent surveys show that over the long term the best investment trusts have performed as well as, if not better than, the best unit trusts and the share indices generally.
- The net asset value discount is an important factor in deciding whether or not to buy. Disastrous falls to as much as 40 per cent discount in the past have unnerved investors, and as a result, the stock market as a whole may not always do justice to investment trusts' performance and potential.
- It's one area where you may be able to beat the experts, if you are careful.

Investment trusts: Summary

SAFETY

Will the capital be repaid in full?	Depends on market.
Are the investments officially regulated?	Yes.
Is the capital protected against inflation?	Depends on market.

AVAILABILITY	Fair.

METHOD

How do you invest?	Through stockbroker.
Are there commission charges?	Yes.
Are there extra charges when you buy and sell?	Spread between bid and offer prices.

INCOME

Is income paid regularly?	Yes. Twice-yearly dividends.

Is it guaranteed?	No.
Are there prospects for capital gains?	Yes.
Is the income high/average/low?	Depends on type and performance of trust.

TAXATION

Is the return assessed for income tax?	Yes.
Is basic rate deducted?	Yes.
Can the tax be reclaimed?	Yes.
Is it assessed for age income relief?	Yes.
Is it assessed for capital gains tax?	Yes.

Chapter 6

Life Insurance and Investment

Since the tax concessions on life insurance premiums were withdrawn in the 1984 Budget, the investment opportunities offered by insurance policies have been considerably reduced. Life insurance companies have been devising new schemes that take account of the new situation, but these now have to be more carefully compared with other types of investment.

The type of policy that covers your car or your home against loss or damage doesn't qualify as an investment, but any insurance scheme that pays you something back, whether or not the catastrophe against which you are insuring happens, may be worth considering.

How safe is your money?

If the insurance company fails, both pensions and insurance are protected in law by the Policy-Holders' Protection Act. The Policy-Holders' Protection Board makes sure that up to 90 per cent of any claims you had outstanding on a short-term policy, such as a car insurance, will be paid up. For a long-term investment policy, such as life insurance or pension, you get 90 per cent of what was promised under the terms of the agreement, as long as the promises were reasonable.

Friendly societies, which may offer insurance and pension plans, are not covered by the Board, but they are supervised by the Registrar of Friendly Societies and should not therefore get into difficulties.

There is very little chance that an insurance-linked investment offering a guaranteed return will fail to come up with what was promised, which is why guaranteed returns tend to be on the low side. However, investments with insurance companies all depend on the skill of the investment managers to provide a high level of return on your money. Those that are directly linked to the price of stocks and shares in the stock market are not protected against loss caused by a fall in the price at the time you cash in your policy. They are subject to the same risks as any other stock market investment. Some companies do much better than others in this respect, so look at the performance tables published regularly in magazines like *Planned Savings* before you choose a company.

Is there any limit on investment?

Anyone can take out life insurance – at a price. Where the investment is linked to life insurance, your age and your state of health will almost certainly be taken into account, except for special policies which pay lower rates and give less insurance cover. There is no limit to the amount of insurance investment you can have, unlike car or property insurance, where there is no point over-insuring, because you won't get back more than the value if you have to claim. There may be minimum or maximum amounts for investment in any one scheme.

If you are taking out any kind of life assurance-linked policy it is important to read all the small print in the proposal form and answer very fully, as if you fail to disclose some important detail about your health or way of life, this may make the policy invalid, even if no specific question was asked on that point.

How do you invest?

There are four main ways of dealing with insurance companies:

- The insurance company will advertise directly to the public in the press, with a coupon to fill in and send off.
- Insurance companies employ salesmen and have a network of agents to sell their policies to the public. Agents represent one, two or three companies, not more; they may be full- or part-time. Frequently, solicitors, accountants etc may act as part-time agents for a company.
- Insurance brokers exist to act as middlemen between different companies and the public to sell different types of policy. Insurance brokers should have a wide knowledge of the different kinds of policy, and be able to advise on the best one to suit your personal needs. The Insurance Brokers Registration Act 1977 has made it compulsory for anyone calling himself an insurance broker to be registered with the Insurance Brokers Registration Council, which lays down a code of professional conduct. This includes the requirement for professional indemnity insurance, so if brokers give bad advice, you will be able to claim against them with some hope of getting your money back.

Remember that brokers are paid commission by most companies to sell their policies, which may influence the advice they give, and that there is no compulsory professional qualification, as for solicitors or accountants, for example.

● Investment advisers will also recommend insurance investments to their clients and act as agents for selling bonds and other policies.

You can take out life insurance investments either by a series of payments – a *regular payment policy* – or by a lump sum payment, a *single premium policy*. There should be no charge for selling you a policy, but the insurance company will deduct its management charges from the annual increase in the value of your investment.

What return does it provide?

Insurance investments are not really geared towards the payment of interest. They are largely about building up capital. The capital gains are re-invested. However, some investments, such as Income Bonds, do pay a regular income. If you *withdraw* an income from these bonds, you are often cashing in some of the capital increase in the value of the bond you have bought instead of leaving it invested. Some Income Bonds will guarantee a rate of interest over a fairly short-term period, and perhaps pay a bonus at the end, when you get your capital back. The bonus will depend on how well the insurance company did out of its investment during that time. These bonds are usually based on short-term annuities or single premium life insurance policies. They are becoming more popular with insurance companies since the ending of tax concessions on regular payment policies.

How is it taxed?

There are still some tax advantages in investing with life insurance.

● *Premium subsidy* consisted of a subsidy of 15 per cent paid to all policy holders, whether or not they paid tax, as long as the policy was for the benefit of the policy holder or spouse. This has now been withdrawn. Policies taken out before April 1984 continue to receive the subsidy as long as the conditions of the policy are not changed, for example by increasing the length of time the policy runs, or increasing the contributions to gain higher benefits.

Insurance policies bought with a lump sum payment – single

premium policies – have never received tax subsidies. There is now no difference as far as income tax is concerned between paying for your policy with one single payment or by regular premiums.

- *Capital gains tax* is not normally charged on the gains you make from life insurance investments. However, insurance companies may deduct something from the proceeds of a unit-linked policy to cover their liability for capital gains tax on future profits on sales of their investments. Alternatively, they may take this into account when fixing the price of units. The amount will be less than the standard rate of capital gains tax, because insurance companies will not normally be selling investments to pay out on policies.

- *Corporation tax* is not paid by insurance companies. They pay tax at a special rate of $37\frac{1}{2}$ per cent on their profits, which gives them an advantage over investments which have no similar tax concession.

- *Income tax.* If you take an income out of an investment linked to life insurance you do not have to pay basic rate tax on it, as this is accounted for by the company at their special rate. You cannot reclaim this if you are a non-taxpayer.

If you keep a regular payments policy for 10 years, or until its full term, any gain from it is *not* assessed for investment income surcharge or higher rates of income tax, and does not affect age income relief.

However, you will be assessed for higher rates of income tax and age income relief on gains and withdrawals from life insurance-linked investments in the following cases:

Gains from a single premium policy whenever you cash it in;
Gains from a regular payments policy if you cash it in before 10 years or three-quarters of its term is up (whichever is the sooner);
If you receive an income from the investment of more than 5 per cent of its value.

In these cases higher rate taxpayers have to pay the difference between the basic rate and any extra tax due. You could also lose age income relief if these gains push your income above the allowance.

If any tax is due you can claim *top-slicing* relief. This is calculated by adding up the sum received when you cash the policy in and any income taken during its life, and deducting what you paid for the policy to give the *gross gain*. Then divide the gross gain by the number of years you held the policy to give the *average gain*. The average gain is added to your taxable income in the year you cash in the policy to decide what rate of tax you pay on the gross gain.

Example
You buy a single premium property bond for £10,000 and take an income of £500 a year from it for 10 years. Then you cash it in for £15,000. Altogether you have received:

10 × £500	£ 5,000
Repayment	£15,000
	£20,000
Less what you paid	£10,000
Gross gain	£10,000
Divide by 10 to give average gain	£ 1,000

When £1000 is added to your income for the final year of the policy, it puts you into the 40 per cent tax bracket, so you pay the difference between the basic rate and 40 per cent, ie 10 per cent on the whole £10,000 gain: a total of £1000 income tax. You can see that top slicing saves you tax as otherwise you could have to pay:

40 per cent on £2,300	£ 920
45 per cent on £4,000	£1,800
50 per cent on £3,700	£1,850
£10,000	£4,570
Less 29 per cent already paid	£2,900
	£1,670

Unfortunately you are not given these concessions when the calculation for age allowance is made; the whole amount of the gain has to be added to your income in the year you cash in the bond. You may be able to avoid this extra liability if you do not need to cash the bond in when it expires, by postponing the date of encashment until your income is lower.

If you cash in a policy which received the 15 per cent premium subsidy during its first four years, the government may want some of its subsidy back. The insurance company will deduct this *clawback* from the proceeds.

What types of investment are there?

There are two main groups of life insurance-linked investments: those where the main purpose is protection for your family with the added bonus of a lump sum payment when the scheme comes to an end, and those which are really investment schemes first and foremost, and which you would not choose if family protection was your main aim. Whole life and endowment policies belong mostly to the first group; unit-linked life insurance and bond schemes to the second group, but there is some overlap.

The simplest form of life insurance scheme is *term* insurance, by which you agree to pay premiums for a fixed period, and if you die in that time the insurance company (or *life office*) pays out a fixed sum to your heirs. If you do not die, you get nothing back at all just as no fire insurance is paid if your house doesn't catch fire. These schemes can be very cheap, the cost depending on your age and state of health. They are not investments but insurance pure and simple.

Schemes which pay out at the end of a fixed period, if you have not died in the meantime, *are* to be considered as investments, and judged by the same rules as any other investment scheme.

Whole life schemes

These are the cheapest. You agree to pay fixed premiums either for the rest of your life, or until you are, say, 65, in return for which the company pays out a fixed sum on your death. They can be *non-profit*, or preferably, *with profit*, in which case a bonus is added to the fixed sum, depending on the success of the company's investment over the years.

The difference between these and *term* insurance is that you can cash them in after a few years, but the cash-in value is likely to be quite small until you have had the policy a long time. The increase in the capital might be as little as 2 per cent a year, even with bonuses. Although they are cheap they are not very good value.

Endowment policies

With these, you pay premiums over a fixed period of years, and at the end of that time, the insurance company pays you back a guaranteed lump sum. If you die before the term is up, the company pays the lump sum to your heirs. These can be *non-profit*, where the total sum you will get back is fixed in advance, or *with profits*, which guarantees a smaller lump sum but you get regular bonuses, known as reversionary bonuses, added to your investment. Bonuses can't be taken back once they have been granted. There may also be a *terminal bonus* at the end of the contract.

The bonuses depend on the success the company's investment managers have had over the years. There are government regulations about the valuation of the company's assets and how bonuses are decided. If you cash in your policy early the return is likely to be rather low; you may get nothing at all if you cash in during the first two years, and as little as 2 or 3 per cent in the third or fourth years. If you want to stop paying, you can decide to make it *paid up* – freeze it at the current level instead of cashing it in – without adding any more premiums. The company may make an extra charge if you do this in the early years of a policy, and some companies will not allow you to make a policy paid up during the first two years.

Flexible endowment policies are the same as with-profit policies, but you are guaranteed a fixed repayment value at the end of part of the term, say 10 years for a 20-year policy. You can either cash in then, or continue investing, so that your guaranteed sum continues to increase. You may be able to cash in part of the policy instead of the whole amount.

Variable life plans

These are a new development which allow you to vary the protection and savings elements in your policy according to your family or other circumstances. When you take the policy out, you decide how much straight life insurance protection you need for your dependants in case you die, and how much you can afford to pay in regular premiums. You then pay this regular amount to the insurance company which puts part of the premium towards the life cover, and the rest into one of its funds to build up a capital sum. Each year you can decide how much goes towards protection and how much is invested in funds. You can increase the premiums in line with inflation. The tax rules are rather complicated but these schemes are worth looking into if you want to provide for a family and save for the future, without constantly having to take out new or different policies.

Unit-linked life insurance
(investment bonds, bond funds)

Unit-linked life insurance investments are based on the same principles as unit and investment trusts; they take money from a number of investors and in return offer units in a fund which spreads the risk and the opportunities for growth of capital and income over a range of stocks and shares. You pay the premiums, and in return, as well as your investment, there is the added bonus of life insurance cover. The value of your investment goes up and down with the stock market, and also depends on the skill with which the insurance company manages the funds.

Like any investment involving stocks and shares there is a *bid* price and an *offer* price for units: you buy from the company at the offer price and sell it back at the bid price, and the difference between the two – the *spread* – covers the management's charges and profit. The prices of all the leading funds are quoted regularly in the financial press. The proportion of your premium that goes towards buying units depends on your age and how much, if any, life insurance protection (a lump sum to your heirs in case you die before you cash in the units) you want the plan to provide. The management also deducts annual charges – about 0.75-1 per cent of the value of your investment in the fund. However, during the early years of an investment plan of this kind, there may be much heavier charges than this, either because fewer units are being allocated to your share, or because there are special charging rates for so-called 'capital' units during the first two years. So it pays to read the small print, and to look at comparisons of the returns on these schemes published regularly in magazines like *Planned Savings*. Over the age of 60 or so, you get less life cover and the proportion allocated to units increases.

You can make your investment either by buying in with a single payment or by regular payments up to 20 years or so. There may be a minimum holding of 100-200 units, or a minimum regular payment of £10-£20.

Because any gains made from single premium policies are assessable for higher rates of tax, there is no restriction on how many you can hold, and how long you have to keep them. The insurance companies may deduct extra charges if you withdraw your money in the very early years. The longer you keep your money in the investment, the lower the charges are as a proportion of the value.

With savings plans, the regular premiums you contribute to the plan are used to buy the agreed amount of life cover, and the remainder (less charges) goes towards the purchase of units at the going rate that month. To some extent, this evens out the ups and downs of the stock market, because your money buys more units when prices are low. This should average out some of the risk of diminishing the value of your savings because of changes in market prices. If you withdraw your money in the early years, you face the probability of heavy penalties, and are unlikely to get back the gross value of the premiums you have paid in. Some plans provide for the deduction of as much as 40 per cent of the premiums in the first two years.

With unit-linked investment you always need to be careful about when you buy and (especially) sell the units, as if you buy when the market is high and sell when it is low, you can lose quite a lot of capital. Make sure that you have some flexibility about the date when the investment is cashed in.

If you pick a unit-linked scheme you then have to decide whether you want:

- High life insurance cover more than income or large increases in the value of your investment (high protection plans). (Unit-linked insurance is not the best way of achieving this; you will probably be better off with term insurance and another kind of investment.)
- High rate of increase in your investment with low life insurance (capital growth plans);
- High income during the term of the investment (high yield plans);
- A combination of all these (standard plans).

Once you have made this decision there is still plenty of choice. Most insurance companies will offer you a choice of funds in which to hold your units. The main groups are:

Managed funds, a mixture of equities, property and fixed-income investments: should produce a safe, if unspectacular, return.

Property funds which invest in office blocks, property shares etc. The fund needs to be very large to cope with the fluctuations of the property market where each investment may be worth millions of pounds. Even then, property funds are more risky than most other funds.

Equity funds invest in shares generally, or in particular kinds of share.

Fixed interest funds which invest in gilts and other loan stocks.

Cash funds which invest in currency, short-term deposits of cash at banks, and with local authorities etc.

International funds where the money is invested in companies operating abroad, sometimes in specific areas.

Switching

Like the unit trust companies, most insurance companies offering these investments will allow switching of your units from one fund to another at lower cost than buying new units. This means that you can influence how well (or badly) your investment does, by choosing the right moment to switch from a fund that is at its peak, so the units have a high value, to another fund that you believe to be about to do better, so that its units are undervalued at present. You can't afford to make too many mistakes as you could lose on both the swings and the roundabouts if you constantly switch at the wrong state of the market.

Income and other bonds
(guaranteed income bonds, growth bonds)

These are various bond schemes offered by insurance companies and friendly societies which use different combinations of single premium endowment insurance policies, and short-term annuities (see p. 90) to produce investments linked to bond funds and sometimes direct investment in gold mines, oil wells etc. Some of these may guarantee a fixed income over the short term, and you get your investment back with or without a bonus at the end of the term, or they may offer capital growth with the opportunity to withdraw some of the projected increase as income during the term.

There is often a minimum investment, say £1000. You cannot usually cash in your bond before the term is up. Some of these schemes are able to offer high rates of interest and capital growth because they are run by offshore companies or use offshore trusts based in countries where taxation is lower. As they are not subject to British government regulations there is a greater element of risk in investing in them. Subsidiaries of well-known and well-established British groups operating offshore are the safest bet. It's very important to read carefully the prospectuses of schemes offering very high rates, and to watch out for words like 'projected' increase, 'assuming' that your units grow at x per cent etc, otherwise you may be in for a disappointment.

Life insurance linked to building societies

Before the premium subsidy was abolished, these schemes could be used to capitalise on the tax advantages of life insurance and building societies at the same time. There is no longer any particular point to the linked schemes, although plans already taken out before abolition can continue to run.

Friendly society bonds
(family bonds)

Friendly societies have special tax advantages because they can run funds which pay no tax at all on their own investments, while gains under their life insurance-linked policies are free of all tax, including investment income surcharge and higher tax rates. On the other hand, because of these advantages, the Inland Revenue place restrictions on the amount you can save. Since 1984 there has been a clampdown on various schemes designed to avoid tax. There is now a limit of £9 a month, or £100 a year per person investing. The amount of life insurance cover is limited to £750.

There are heavy penalties if you withdraw your investment before 10 years are up, though you may be able to make the policy *paid up* or *frozen*. Friendly society rules mean that if you cash in before the 10-year term is completed, you cannot get back more than your premiums – no interest. There are extra penalties if you cash in during the first two years. There may be heavy 'discontinuance' charges, and some policies pay back nothing at all in the first two years.

Most societies offer a lump-sum payment scheme whereby you pay a lump sum into a building society and receive building society interest on the amount remaining in the account as the premiums are withdrawn into the policy. This interest is taxed at source at the composite rate.

The friendly societies offer building society linked, unit trust linked and endowment policies. They are good value for taxpayers, especially those paying higher rates who are sure of keeping up the payments and don't want their money back early.

The new 'baby bonds' which allow taxpayers to take out savings schemes for people under 18 have already fallen foul of the Inland Revenue in some cases, though existing policies are safe.

Other schemes may be on offer which combine some of the advantages of friendly societies and insurance policies, without relying on the full tax concessions available to friendly societies.

Index linking and insurance

When inflation is low, there is not much point in promoting index-linked schemes, but there are various ways in which insurance companies can compete with other index-linked investments. Some of the companies have offered index-linked bonds based on gilt funds. These normally run for five years and offer index-linking plus a bonus at the end of the term, with a minimum investment from £500 up to a maximum of £50,000. If you withdraw the money early, the amount received depends on market prices and is not guaranteed. The return would be assessed for higher rates of tax, investment income surcharge, and age relief.

You can also buy an annuity (see p. 108) linked to the Retail Price Index, or you could use a lump sum to buy an annuity the proceeds from which could buy into an SAYE (see p. 30) contract. However, these schemes are relatively expensive, and other forms of investment show a higher return when inflation is not rising fast.

Points to watch

- The insurance companies employ highly sophisticated salesmen who, naturally, stress the advantages of their schemes in their sales talk. It's up to you to read the small print very carefully and watch out for snags.
- Insurance-linked investments are mainly designed for the long term. Charges and penalties for cashing in early may be a nasty shock. Make sure they are spelt out.
- Check up on the level of management charges the company makes – these vary quite a lot.
- When you are choosing a unit-linked investment find out what the charges are for switching.
- There have been some spectacular failures of offshore companies offering insurance-linked investments.
- Check what the policy pays out if you die before the policy is paid up. For example, what interest is paid on your contributions.

- Don't take the easy way out and accept whatever the agent who rings up on spec or advertises through the post, offers you. Compare different companies and don't be shy about asking for quotations from different brokers before you make your decision.
- It's as well not to put all your pension and life insurance investments into the same kind of scheme. Ring the changes and cover your losses.

Summary

Regular payment policies

SAFETY

Will the capital be repaid in full?	Yes.
Are the investments officially regulated?	Yes.
Is the capital protected against inflation?	Depends on scheme.

AVAILABILITY	Excellent.

METHOD

How do you invest?	Through agent or direct with insurance company.
Are there commission charges?	Deducted from funds.
Are there extra charges when you buy and sell?	No. Spread between bid and offer prices in unit-linked plans.

INCOME

Is income paid regularly?	No.
Is it guaranteed?	Depends on scheme.
Are there prospects for capital gains?	Yes.
Is the income high/average/low?	Depends on scheme.

TAXATION

Is the return assessed for income tax?	Not if policy kept for 10 years.

Is basic rate deducted?	Yes.
Can the tax be reclaimed?	No.
Is it assessed for age income relief?	Not if policy kept for 10 years.
Is it assessed for capital gains tax?	No.

Single premium policies

SAFETY

Will the capital be repaid in full?	Yes.
Are the investments officially regulated?	Yes.
Is the capital protected against inflation?	Depends on scheme.

AVAILABILITY	Excellent.

METHOD

How do you invest?	Through agent or direct with insurance company.
Are there commission charges?	Deducted from funds.
Are there extra charges when you buy and sell?	No. Spread between bid and offer prices in unit-linked plans.

INCOME

Is income paid regularly?	No, except income bonds.
Is it guaranteed?	Yes – income bonds.
Are there prospects for capital gains?	Yes.
Is the income high/average/low?	Depends on scheme.

TAXATION

Is the return assessed for income tax?	Yes.
Is basic rate deducted?	Yes.
Can the tax be reclaimed?	No.
Is it assessed for age income relief?	Yes.
Is it assessed for capital gains tax?	No.

Chapter 7

Pensions

Life insurance and pensions are inextricably linked, because the same companies offer the schemes, and the principles are very similar, although there are some important differences. The tax concessions they receive make all pension schemes very tax-efficient investments and everyone should have one if they can.

Personal pension plans

How safe is your money?
The Policy-Holders' Protection Act protects pensions in the same way as life insurance (see p. 88).

Are there any limits on investment?
Unfortunately you cannot normally take out your own personal pension plan unless one of the following conditions applies:

- You are self-employed;
- You have enough freelance earnings outside your regular job to make it worthwhile;
- You have two or more jobs and at least one has no pension scheme;
- You are *not* a member of a company pension scheme.

However, this still leaves large numbers of people who do not realise that they could be building up valuable investments through a personal pension plan.

How do you invest?
The problem is not finding a pension fund to suit you, but deciding which one to use. If you have plenty of stamina, you can approach several different brokers, agents, and companies direct, though you may be overwhelmed by the high pressure salesmanship that follows. It's best to get as much factual information as

you can from performance tables, press comment etc, before you talk to any company. The *Financial Times* publishes an annual Self-Employed Pensions Handbook, which has all the information you could possibly need on this, but it costs £19. It might be in a good specialist reference library.

The company you choose will want to know about your health as well as your financial circumstances, especially if some life cover is included in the scheme.

You can either pay by regular contributions, or by a single premium. There will probably be a minimum sum, say £10 a month for regular payment. Many companies prefer you to pay yearly or half-yearly, and may make a small extra charge if you want to pay monthly. There may be a maximum payment into any one scheme. You continue paying until you retire – or for a fixed period, say 20 years – and the amount you get then depends on how long you have been paying into the scheme.

There may be a minimum payment of £250-£500 for single premium payments into a scheme. You can make additional payments into the same scheme, or different schemes, as and when it suits you. This has two advantages: you can pick and choose the best buys, and the best time in the market to buy; and you can vary your payments to take account of your qualifying earnings each year.

You normally have to state when you intend to retire, and this must be within the age range 60 to 75 unless your job is one that has a fixed early retirement date. You don't *have* to stop work when you begin receiving the pension. You can change your mind about the date with most policies, as long as it's within the permitted age range.

If you *have* to retire early because of ill-health, you can start taking the benefits straight away, but they will be lower than if you stay the course to the normal age.

If you die before retirement most policies pay a lump sum to your heirs. If you want this to include interest on the premiums you have paid, the pension you would get is lower than it would otherwise be.

If you want to, or have to, stop paying before you reach the retiring age, you cannot claim a refund of contributions. They remain *frozen* in the scheme until you retire, though they will still increase along with the rest of the fund. You may be able to use them as security for a loan (see p. 111).

The company may make an extra charge if you freeze a policy in the early stages.

Most schemes will allow you to miss one or two payments, or to make them up later, but there is normally a time limit on this. The insurance company makes an annual management charge against your investment in the scheme to cover its costs. This depends on the type of scheme you choose.

What return does it provide?

You do not get interest from a pension scheme. All the profits are re-invested in the fund to provide the largest possible sum on retirement.

How is it taxed?

The contributions you make to a personal pension plan are tax free up to a certain level. You deduct them from your income before tax so they reduce your tax bill at its highest rate; therefore, the more tax you pay the better bargain it is. If you pay tax at the 45 per cent rate, for instance, pension contributions of £1000 could cost you only £550 because of the tax you would save.

This tax concession applies to pension contributions up to a maximum of 17½ per cent of your *relevant* earnings, 20 per cent or more if you were born before 1934. (These tax rules may be changed from year to year.) The earnings that qualify for the concession are your profits less allowances if you are self-employed, your profits from freelance earnings, or your salary less allowances if you are in a non-pension job. If you have two jobs, one of which qualifies, and your total income puts you in a higher tax bracket, you will still get the contributions free of the highest rate of tax you pay.

Example
You earn a taxable income of £10,000 a year from a job in a company, plus £5000 a year from writing novels. You can take out a personal pension plan and get tax-free contributions on 17½ per cent of £5000 = £875. This would be deducted from your top rate of tax at 40 per cent.

In addition to this tax relief, the income you receive from your pension scheme when you reach retiring age is taxed as earned, rather than investment, income and if you take a lump sum this is tax free.

Moreover, the companies managing pension funds do not pay capital gains or income tax on their pension fund investments, so they can offer higher rates of return than companies which do pay those taxes.

Backdating pension fund contributions

You may not have taken up the full amount of tax-free pension contributions allowed in the past, perhaps because you could not afford to at the time. If you can now afford to do so, you can go back six years and make up these contributions to the maximum level permitted at that time (the amount you pay in backdated contributions is deducted from your taxable income in the year in which you actually pay the contribution.

So if you did not take out a personal pension plan until 1983, although you had been self-employed for the past 10 years, go back (in the 1985/6 tax year) to 1979/80, work out what you could have paid in pension contributions then, and make them up out of this year's income. If you can't afford to make up the whole six years at once, you can do it year by year, always paying the earliest year's contribution first. (Unfortunately, the insurance company won't backdate the payment into the scheme as if you had paid it then, but you can't have everything.)

On top of this you can ask the tax inspector to pre-date any contribution from the present tax year to the past one, if you have some spare allowance left. This can also help you make up lost contributions. It's a complicated procedure but the tax man or your accountant can advise you. Too many people leave their pension planning until late in the day; these tax provisions help you make up for lost time.

What types of investment are there?

You have to choose at the outset the *kind* of scheme you will pay into. The choices are very similar to life insurance. You can have a *non-profit plan*, where you get a guaranteed pension fixed from the start, which may be low because of the uncertainty of how investment will turn out over the period. It would be a good buy if you thought interest rates were about to fall and stay low for your foreseeable future.

With-profits plans have a lower guaranteed pension, but you share in the profits made by the fund over the years, and every year, or every three years, a reversionary bonus is added to your guaranteed pension, which cannot then be withdrawn by the company. You may also get a *terminal* bonus on retirement, which will depend on the state of the investment fund at that time.

With *unit-linked pensions* you buy units in the various funds run by the insurance company. As for insurance (see p. 96), you have a choice of funds, usually between property, equity, fixed-interest, cash, managed, and international funds. You can normally switch your investment from one fund to another for a small charge.

The value of the pension you get depends on the value of the units when it comes to retirement, so the state of the market at that time may make quite a difference to your pension.

(NB. You cannot cash in these units as you can with a similar life insurance unit-linked scheme.)

Flexible pension plans offered by some companies allow you to vary the amount of contributions each year to some extent, and to miss contributions (up to a limit) without penalty. So if you are not sure whether your relevant earnings will allow you to keep up regular contributions, a plan like this might be more suitable.

Deposit administration schemes allow you to place your money on deposit with the insurance company which pays interest and adds it to your investment at regular intervals. There may be a guaranteed minimum rate of interest.

You cannot lose any of the original sum, but how fast it increases depends on interest rates.

Whatever scheme you choose, when the time comes to retire, or when the agreed term comes to an end, your investment in the scheme is used to buy you a pension. How high this is depends on the type of scheme, and how well the insurance company has managed its investments.

Because some pension funds may offer a better deal than others for certain kinds of pension arrangement, many plans include an option to switch your investment to another company at retirement age, and buy your actual pension from them. This is called an *open market option*. Few people take advantage of it because it looks too complicated, but it can markedly affect the level of your pension, because different companies offer different annuity rates, so check what the rates are (see p. 109) before you decide.

You are faced with many options when it comes to deciding how your accumulated pension investment should be spent. These are some of the more important choices you can make:

● Take a cash lump sum which can be up to three times the value of the remaining pension you will receive from that scheme;
● Receive a pension at a fixed rate until you die;
● Receive a pension increasing at, say 5 per cent a year, compounded;

- Receive a pension related to a unit-linked fund;
- Have the pension paid on a *joint-life or survivor* basis with your spouse, which means that if one of you dies, the other continues to receive all or some of the pension;
- Continue to work and contribute payments after the retirement date has been reached and put off receiving the benefits (not after 75);
- Put off receiving the pension and freeze your pension at its present amount; this will go on increasing in line with the rest of the fund, but you do not pay any more in.

Not all of these possibilities will be available in every pension scheme, and if any seem particularly important to you, check before taking out an investment whether or not it offers those options. What you choose will affect the amount of pension you receive.

It makes sense not to put all your pension money into the same kind of scheme, but to go for a judicious mixture, according to your own personal circumstances.

Annuities

When you buy an annuity you are parting with your capital in return for guaranteed payments, either for a fixed period, or until death. Pensions are a form of annuity, because you are trading in a lump sum accumulated over the years for a pension guaranteed until your death.

Annuities that you have to buy as part of a pension scheme are known as compulsorily purchased annuities. You can buy an annuity without having contributed to a pension scheme, and short-term annuities form an important part of some income bond schemes.

Unless it is part of a pension scheme, you are unlikely to get much of a bargain out of buying an annuity to provide for your old age until you are past retirement age, because the rates you get in return for your lump sum are carefully calculated by age and sex. They may be good value for someone over 70, say, worried about the effect of inflation on their capital.

How safe is your money?
Annuities are protected in the same way as other insurance investments, by the Policy-Holders' Protection Act.

Are there any limits on investment?
You can invest as much as you like in annuities; there are no legal limitations.

How do you invest?
Insurance companies are keen competitors in this field, and you would need to compare the rates they were offering before deciding which to buy. Rates are published regularly in magazines like *Money Management* and *Planned Savings*, but these may be out of date by the time you see them.

A new development is Murray Noble's Open Market Annuity 'hotline' service, which offers independent, impartial advice about the best available going rates for annuities, and will also advise on the different types of annuity options on offer. You can contact the Hotline on 01-242 2343.

The Quotel Computerised Information Service gives details of the rates offered by over 100 companies. This is made available to insurance brokers subscribing to the Quotel service. Quotel does not itself recommend insurance companies or best buys to individuals, but can put you in touch with a local broker using the service. You can get more information about how the system works from Quotel Insurance Service, GSI UK Ltd, Stanhope Road, Camberley, Surrey GU15 3PS; tel: 0276 62155.

What return does it provide?
The regular payment you get back from an annuity ought to provide a higher rate of return than you could get from interest on other investments if it is to be worthwhile giving up your capital. So you need to compare it with what you would get from gilts or a similar fixed-interest investment, or from index-linked investments.

When interest rates are high you stand a better chance of getting a high return, because the companies will have to offer a good rate to persuade anyone to buy, and the rate is then fixed for as long as you live.

Rates vary from month to month, or even from day to day, so keep an eye on them before laying out your capital.

How is it taxed?
If you *have* to buy an annuity, as you would under most pension schemes, you pay tax on all the income you receive from it at

earned income rates. The insurance company deducts tax at the basic rate, and you can reclaim this if you are a basic rate tax-payer. Income from annuities has to be declared for investment income surcharge, and may affect higher rates of tax and age income relief.

However, if you *choose* to buy an annuity with some of your capital, different tax rules apply. Part of what you get back from an annuity is regarded by the tax inspector as a repayment of capital that you have lent the insurance company, so this capital part is tax free.

It is this feature of annuities that makes them so useful to companies offering guaranteed income bonds, as buying a short-term annuity means that you do not have to pay tax on part of the income you receive from the bond.

The remainder of the payment is counted as investment, or un-earned, income, and may affect your liability for higher rates of tax and age income relief. Basic rate tax is accounted for by the company before it pays you. Non-taxpayers get a slightly higher payment to compensate for this.

What types of investment are there?

You can get *joint-life and survivor* annuities; annuities that *guarantee payment* for a fixed period regardless of whether you die before the period is up; *increasing annuities* which increase at an agreed rate over the years; or *unit-linked* annuities, tied to the value of funds of your choice. *Short-term annuities*, which often form part of income bond schemes, are designed to produce guaranteed incomes over a fairly short period – one to five years (see p. 97). The rates you receive from these will probably be lower than those from annuities paid until death, because the number of payments is fixed.

Additional voluntary contributions (AVCs)

You may not realise that even if you are in a company pension scheme it is possible to top this up with additional voluntary contributions, as long as you are still below the Inland Revenue maximum of 15 per cent of your earnings. You get income tax relief on the extra contributions you pay. You agree to invest a regular amount with the organisation offering the AVC scheme. This may be a building society, which will pay a high rate of interest gross (without deducting tax) which is re-invested in the scheme, or a life insurance company offering the ordinary life insurance endowment type policy, with guaranteed bonus, or a unit-linked fund, or a conventional pension scheme. The AVC fund is given precisely the same tax concessions as regular pension funds, so the rate of return is higher than for ordinary investments. When you retire, you receive either a tax-free lump sum, which can be used to buy a pension that is taxed as earned income, or an annual income – also taxed at earned income rate – or a combination of the two.

The snag is that your company has to be prepared to offer an AVC scheme; you cannot do it yourself. As it costs the company very little, it ought to be provided if you ask, and many companies do already provide facilities for AVCs, though employees may not be aware of this.

Like other pension schemes you cannot withdraw your investment, though you might be able to borrow on it if you needed cash urgently.

Some insurance companies, Equitable Life, for example, offer top-up schemes open to anyone meeting certain conditions. These are usually more suitable for highly-paid executives who are not taking up all the concessions allowed by the Inland Revenue.

Loanback

To read some of the publicity for loanback facilities you might think that the insurance companies are giving money away; in fact they are lending you your own money back. In other words, the insurance company will make you a loan based on what you have paid into a pension or life assurance scheme. This is an answer to the major problem with investment in pension schemes, that the money, once invested, is inaccessible until the investor retires.

In the past, insurance companies have usually been prepared to lend you a proportion of any guaranteed sum you are entitled to receive at the end of a pension or life assurance scheme. Normally you pay interest on the loan, and the lump sum you have borrowed is deducted from the total due to you at the end of the term. Loanback is a more sophisticated version of this, as instead of borrowing money from the insurance company, you are in effect borrowing the money from your own personal pension fund, and the interest you pay goes back into *your* fund, not to the insurance company. The insurance company deducts a management charge, so it costs you something. When you come to retire, you will have less capital invested in your pension fund because you have already taken some of it out (unless you pay it back in the meantime). Although the amount lent has been earning interest from you, this may be less than it would have earned had it remained in the company's fund.

The company may require security in addition to the pension scheme to guarantee the loan, eg the deeds of your home.

If you really want to be clever, you can borrow by loanback in order to take advantage of the tax concession that allows you to backdate contributions to your pension fund. Because these contributions are tax deductible, it may be profitable to do this, even allowing for the cost of the loan. Get your accountant or adviser to work out the cost for you.

Points to watch

We've tried here to give the basic facts about a very complicated business, to help you follow what the experts are talking about.

- Make sure that the pension fund spells out the policy on charging, and that any penalties are clearly explained.
- Keep a running total of your investment or pension plans to warn you when you reach the 17½ per cent maximum for the tax concessions that make pension funds extra profitable.
- If you borrow money on an insurance or pension policy, keep up the interest payments or they will be compounded and at the end you will have far more to pay than you need.
- Personal pension planning is one form of investment where the sales pressure is very keen. Just because it is easy, don't assume that it is always the best way of saving. Term life insurance, coupled with some other savings plan, may be better in the long run.
- Shop around for the best bargain; don't hurry into any decisions.

Summary

Personal pension plans

SAFETY

Will the capital be repaid in full?	Yes.
Are the investments officially regulated?	Yes.
Is the capital protected against inflation?	To some extent.

AVAILABILITY	Excellent.

METHOD

How do you invest?	Through agent or direct with insurance company.
Are there commission charges?	No. Management charges on fund.
Are there extra charges when you buy and sell?	No.

INCOME

Is income paid regularly?	Yes, on retirement.
Is it guaranteed?	Depends on scheme.
Are there prospects for capital gains?	Yes.
Is the income high/average/low?	High.

TAXATION

Is the return assessed for income tax?	Yes.
Is basic rate deducted?	No.
Can the tax be reclaimed?	—
Is it assessed for age income relief?	Yes.
Is it assessed for capital gains tax?	No.

Annuities (compulsorily purchased)

SAFETY

Will the capital be repaid in full?	No.

Are the investments officially regulated?	Yes.
Is the capital protected against inflation?	No.
AVAILABILITY	Good.
METHOD	
How do you invest?	Through insurance company.
Are there commission charges?	No.
Are there extra charges when you buy and sell?	—
INCOME	
Is income paid regularly?	Yes.
Is it guaranteed?	Yes.
Are there prospects for capital gains?	No.
Is the income high/average/low?	High.
TAXATION	
Is the return assessed for income tax?	Yes.
Is basic rate deducted?	Yes.
Can the tax be reclaimed?	Yes.
Is it assessed for age income relief?	Yes.
Is it assessed for capital gains tax?	No.

Annuities (optional)

SAFETY	
Will the capital be repaid in full?	No, except under special income schemes.
Are the investments officially regulated?	Yes.
Is the capital protected against inflation?	No.
AVAILABILITY	Good.

METHOD

How do you invest?	Through insurance company.
Are there commission charges?	No.
Are there extra charges when you buy and sell?	—

INCOME

Is income paid regularly?	Yes.
Is it guaranteed?	Yes.
Are there prospects for capital gains?	No.
Is the income high/average/ low?	High.

TAXATION

Is the return assessed for income tax?	Partly.
Is basic rate deducted?	Yes.
Can the tax be reclaimed?	No – non-taxpayers may get higher rate.
Is it assessed for age income relief?	Yes.
Is it assessed for capital gains tax?	Partly.

Chapter 8

Investing in Things

This is strictly not a field for the novice, unless you like backing outsiders and are sure that you were born under a lucky star. The pitfalls are many, though the profits may be high.

There are three ways you can put your money into *tangibles*, as they are sometimes called, though some are more tangible than others.

Physicals. You can buy the actual objects – gold bars, sacks of coffee, old masters, at the going, or *spot*, price. Then you have to store them, insure them and keep them in good condition. They won't bring you in any income; in fact they cost you money until you sell them, and there's no guarantee that you will be able to sell at a profit.

Futures. You can buy and sell contracts to buy or sell tangibles some time in the future. In this case you never see, and possibly never own, the finished goods; you are gambling that you can out-guess the market as to what the price of gold, copper, or wheat will be in a few months' time. Again, you get no interest on your investment and there is no guarantee that you will make a profit.

One typical use of the futures market is called a *cash and carry* operation. Normally the forward price will be higher than the spot price because of the uncertainty, and because storage and other costs have to be accounted for when the commodity is supplied in the future. So you buy at the spot price and at the same time take out a contract to sell at the forward, higher price – thus guaranteeing a profit, as long as the storage and other costs are less than the difference between the spot and forward prices.

It's not a field for the amateur to dabble in, but a highly professional business, with international markets and time and currency differences as extra complications.

Funds. You can put your money into funds managed by those who claim to be experts and who should know their way around the hazards. The funds may invest in physicals or futures or both, and through their managers' skills and their greater opportunity to spread the risks, should be able to do better than the individual investor. You will still have to decide the right moment to buy into a fund and when to sell your stake. Funds pay interest as well as aiming to provide an increase in the value of your capital. Although you may still lose money if you have to sell at a bad time in the market, you will at least be able to find a buyer to take the units off your hands, which is not always the case with a painting or a few tons of some perishable commodity.

How safe is your money?
Enough has been said already to make it clear that there is very little safety in investing in things. The market in tangibles has never recovered from the boom and (almost) bust of around 1980, when prices which had been climbing steadily for many years suddenly rose sharply and then fell just as sharply.

Tangibles have to be regarded as a long-term investment anyway, except for the market in futures. It's in the long term that you are likely to see the most satisfactory profits.

Another problem is that there is very little statutory regulation of dealings in these kinds of investment. There is nothing comparable to the control the Stock Exchange exercises over member firms and no official funds to compensate investors in cases of fraud or negligence.

Normal company laws operate, but this is not much help if a firm goes bankrupt with thousands of pounds' worth of debts, or offers advice and other services so incompetent as to be positively harmful.

You can reduce the risks by investing in funds rather than physicals, but even then the fluctuations in the value of your investment are likely to be rather alarming. However, if you have enough tucked away in fairly safe investments, and it won't be disastrous if you lose your money, you may think that the chances of making a big profit are worth the risks.

Are there any limits on investment?
Anyone can invest in tangibles, providing they have enough money; it is unlikely to be worthwhile unless you can commit quite large sums, anything from £10,000 to £25,000, though the minimum amounts for the various funds may be lower. There is no limit to the amount you can invest. There are no restrictions about holding gold or foreign currency, but this can change.

How do you invest?

You will almost always have to go through a broker or dealer, in the same way as you would to buy stocks and shares. The broker will charge commission, quite high in some cases. Although you are advised always to go to a sound and reputable dealer, it is not always easy to know how to find one. The best firms tend to prefer to get new clients by personal recommendation, which makes it difficult for new arrivals. Board of Trade regulations often forbid dealers to advertise, because of the feeling that advertising may attract small investors who might not know enough about the risks involved. You tend to be safer with funds managed by one of the big well-known British groups who are also active in insurance, pensions, finance houses etc. Membership of the trade associations may be some guide – they will be able to give you a list of their member firms.

The length of time a firm has been trading may be of some significance, though you ought not to rule out newcomers solely on that account, as they may be just the people to liven up a dull market. You could ask your bank to get a banker's reference and then ask the bank manager to explain just what those guarded comments really mean. Probably the best plan is to talk to other people interested in the same field and read all you can in the financial and specialist press. Then, when you have a short list of firms to contact, get the answers to some searching questions on such details as past performance, costs and charges, the company's attitude to gearing – borrowing to buy more assets – and, most important question of all, to what extent are clients' funds kept separate from the firm's own money, so that if the firm does go bankrupt, the client doesn't lose everything.

Once you have been accepted by a broker, or formed a good relationship with a dealer, you give him your order to buy and sell, just as for a stockbroker.

What return does it provide?

You are not likely to get an income out of investment in tangibles. The attraction is the chance of increasing the value of your capital, though some of the funds may make regular interest payments. It can't be stressed too much that there are no guarantees, either that your investment will be worth more, or that you will get all your money back.

How is it taxed?

The tax position about tangibles is very confusing, because much depends on how the Inland Revenue view your dealings. If it is thought you are carrying on a business by trading in gold or antiques or whatever, you will be assessed on your profits for income tax, at basic and, if necessary, higher rates. They will be taken into account for age income relief. If not, your gains will be assessed for capital gains tax, except that sales of antiques and jewellery are free of capital gains tax if the item is sold for under £3000.

Any income you receive from funds will be taxed as income in the usual way, and will be assessed for investment income surcharge, higher rates of tax and age income relief. You will almost certainly need the help of an accountant to sort out your tax if you are going into tangibles in a big way.

What types of investment are there?

There are many different kinds of tangibles in which you might invest. Here is a brief description of some of them.

Commodities

London is a big centre for trading in raw materials or commodities from all over the world. Leaving aside gold and oil, which are special cases, commodity trading in the City is generally concerned with two main groups: the *metals*, eg copper, lead, tin, silver, zinc; and the *soft commodities* such as barley, cocoa, coffee, cotton, rubber, soy bean products, sugar, wheat and wool. There are separate markets for all these products, each with their own rules and specialist firms.

Commodity markets are run for the benefit of the dealers in commodities, and such rules as they have are designed to protect them rather than outsiders who are looking to make a quick profit; the recent collapse of two big firms of commodity brokers, each losing over £1 million of investors' money, points up the dangers and uncertainties.

In spite of attempts at price agreements, commodity prices are affected by the weather and other natural events; by politics, especially in the developing countries which are often the main suppliers of raw materials; by economic crises; and by the exchange rates which are themselves affected by all these factors.

119

So it's not surprising that the ups and downs of commodity markets are even more pronounced than for other tangibles.

Look at what happened to the price of coffee, for example, in 1985; its chart looks like an outline of one of the more precipitous Alps:

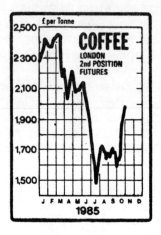

© *Financial Times*

The prices of all the leading commodities are given every day in the financial press.

Commodity physicals. This is no place for the small investor. If you want to buy the actual commodity, the minimum amounts you can deal in may cost anything upwards of £20,000. You then have to pay for storage and insurance until you sell. There is always the possibility that soft commodities in particular will deteriorate before you can sell them, so the risks of losing all your money are even higher than usual.

If you are tempted nevertheless, you would have to find a commodity broker interested in taking on new business. Physical commodities will not pay you any interest, and in the last year or two they have not paid much else either, their price rises have been lagging behind prices generally, and in 1985 they reached a very low level.

Commodity futures. The real interest in commodities for the investor, as distinct from the producer or the manufacturer, is in dealing in futures.

The reason for futures markets is to reduce the risks producers and manufacturers face because of fluctuation in commodity prices. Speculators in futures take on some of this risk in return for the chance of a good profit.

When you take out a *futures contract* you are making a binding agreement to buy or sell the commodity at a fixed price on a fixed date. You are gambling on your opinion of how the market price in that commodity will change in the next few months. There are different rules for different commodities about how far ahead you can deal, but it is usually a matter of months, rather than years. In November 1985, for example, you could buy barley futures at prices ranging from £109.15 a metric tonne for delivery in January 1986, to £114.65 a tonne for delivery in May 1986. If you thought that the price of barley would fall below £114.65 a tonne by May 1986, you could make a futures contract to *sell* at that price, and hope to make a profit on the deal by buying at a lower price to re-sell at £114.65. If you thought that the price would rise, you could contract to *buy* at £114.65 with the hope of re-selling at a higher price.

You have to put down a deposit of about 10 per cent of the contract price at the time of making the contract. But you can lose more than this because if the price changes rapidly in the wrong direction, so your contract is no longer worth very much, your broker will either want you to put up a higher deposit (known as a *margin call*), or insist that you sell the contract immediately for what you can get, though this will mean a loss.

Example

Suppose that in November 1985 you took out a futures contract to buy 1000 tonnes of barley in May 1986 at £114.65 a tonne. You put down a deposit of about £12,000. Suddenly there is an unexpected glut in barley and the price drops to £88.85. You are committed to paying £114,650 in May for grain that is now worth £88,850. You may be able to sell your contract for, say, £10,000 and make an immediate loss of £2000, or you may hang on in the hope that the price will recover. In that case your broker may want another £20,000-£30,000 now, and you may still not recover your money in May. If your contract had been to *sell* at £114.650, you would of course be laughing all the way to the bank.

Futures contracts are different from the *options* discussed on p. 67 because you can let options lapse, without any penalty, or having to take up the option to buy or sell. Futures contracts have no such let-out; you are committed to perform the contract, if you can't sell it to someone else.

You can buy options on futures, which is less risky, and also less profitable, as you have to deduct the cost of the option from any profit on the main deal.

Commodity funds

There are ways you can spread the risk of investing in commodities.

Syndicates. You can join a syndicate in which a group of investors contribute funds which are managed by a commodity broker. Normally, the brokers have complete discretion to manage your money, buying and selling as they choose, so you are very dependent on their skill, and have no say in how the investments are made. You can still lose quite substantially, though the risks should be lower than for the individual.

Commodity trusts. Although UK authorised trusts are not allowed to invest directly in commodities, there are offshore trusts based in tax havens abroad, which deal in commodity physicals and futures. They are on the same lines as unit trusts; your investment buys you a certain number of units in the trust, and you receive either an income from the profits, or an increase in the value of your units, or a combination of the two. The management deducts an annual management charge from the profits and there will be a *spread* between the *bid* price at which the trust will buy back your units and the *offer* price at which they are sold. The price of units depends on commodity prices. The minimum investment is about £1000, sometimes lower.

Unit and investment trusts. To diminish your risk still more you could decide to invest in authorised unit trusts or investment trusts which specialise in the *shares* of commodity companies – for example, something like Henderson Oil and Natural Resources Trust. There is a full account of unit and investment trusts in Chapter 5.

Gold

Gold be damned, said Lord Keynes, the economist, some 60 years ago. He was talking about the pernicious effect gold had on the world economy, which he believed had helped to cause the depression of the 1920s. No doubt those investors who bought gold at $850 an ounce in January 1980 and saw the price fall to below $300 by mid-1982 would have agreed with him. Even the Falklands crisis and the wars in Iran and Lebanon, which should have boosted gold prices, had no immediate effect, and even now, the price rarely goes above $400.

Physicals – solid gold. Up to the present day, despite some alarming fluctuations, gold bullion has managed over the long term to hold its value relative to the cost of living. Whether or not this will continue is something that exercises the best financial brains, and the consensus seems to be that when the market is as low as it has been recently, it may be worth buying gold provided you will not want to sell it in a hurry.

Anyone can buy gold; there are no longer any restrictions about owning gold bars or gold coins, but most small investors will be thinking of coins rather than bars because of the price – a standard gold bar weighing 100 troy ounces is beyond most pockets.

The price of gold is based on the price fixed twice a day on the London Gold Market. This is quoted in US dollars a troy ounce, which weighs about 10 per cent more than an ordinary ounce. On 17 January 1986 the price was $357.25 (about £248) at the morning fixing, and $352.60 (about £244) at the afternoon fixing. If you had bought at the end of November at $234 an ounce, you would have made a profit of about 10 per cent in two months.

The gold coins that investors buy are minted specially; they are not the used coins which are collectors' pieces. The two main types are South African Krugerrands which weigh exactly one troy ounce, and British sovereigns, which weigh just under a quarter of a troy ounce, 0.2354 to be precise. Coins may be sold at a *premium* – a higher price than the gold contained in the coin is worth. On 17 January 1986 the price quoted for Krugerrands was $354, a premium of 0.3 per cent and for new sovereigns $85, a premium of 2.4 per cent. However, you would have had to shop around to find them at this price, because the prices quoted in the press are those for the London market and generally apply to large investors, buying perhaps £1000-worth of coins. If you want to buy a single coin the price will be higher. You can buy coins from the firms on the London Gold Market, who may only deal in large quantities but give the best prices, from the High Street banks (over the counter at some London branches), from a coin dealer, or through your stockbroker. It pays to check the prices at different places before you buy or sell as they vary a lot. The *Krugerrand Directory* issued free by the International Gold Corporation, (Wool House, 6 Carlton House Terrace, London SW1Y 5AE) gives all the facts and figures about Krugerrands, including where and how to buy them from banks and coin dealers.

In April 1982, 15 per cent VAT was imposed on sales of gold

coins, which had previously been exempt. This meant that some people were holding coins they had bought without paying VAT, but new investors had to pay 15 per cent extra on any purchases, which they could not reclaim. So before they had any hope of making a profit on a sale, the gold price had to rise by 15 per cent, just to cover the VAT. As a result, various perfectly legal schemes to avoid payment of VAT have arisen. You can either keep your gold abroad (a popular place being the Channel Islands) because you don't have to pay VAT until you actually receive the coin, or you can swop with someone who wants to sell. You need to take professional advice about the position before buying gold coins through these schemes.

Gold futures. The London Gold Futures Market was opened on 19 April 1982 and closed in 1985, because of uncertainties and lack of business.

Gold funds. You can invest in authorised unit trusts and investment trusts that specialise in shares in gold-mining companies. There are also offshore funds, some offering gold bonds which provide direct investment in gold mines, but you need to be wary about their credentials.

Diamonds and other gems

Diamonds may be a better friend to a girl than a kiss on the hand, but it's very doubtful if they bring much joy to the average investor. There are too many ifs involved in buying any precious stones, unless you have been trained in Hatton Garden. You need expert knowledge to make sure that the stones you are buying are flawless, or indeed what they are claimed to be. A certificate of quality is essential, but even then some certificates are worth more than others, and none is guaranteed infallible.

You have to take into account the huge mark-up dealers may put on the price, perhaps as much as 100 per cent so that the spread between the buying and the selling price can be staggering. There is the question of scarcity value; how long, for example, can De Beers afford to go on buying up the world's surplus diamond production? Although diamonds have been a good investment in the past, they are rather a luxury for the small investor today.

Physicals. There are two kinds of diamond that may be bought for investment. You can buy the kind of stone used for diamond jewellery, which at least gives you the pleasure of wearing or looking at it. You would buy these from a jeweller, a diamond merchant, or at an auction. The problem is that because of dealers' mark-ups you may have considerable problems in selling at a profit or even getting your money back. In spite of the publicity given to sales of some famous stones, you are unlikely to make a profit in anything less than the very long term. People who sell their great-great-aunt's Victorian diamond brooch may be pleasantly surprised at what they receive, but anyone who bought diamond jewellery in the last few years may have to wait a long time for large profits or even to recoup their investment.

Investment diamonds are bought from a diamond investment broker, and you normally never see them because they are stored offshore in a tax haven, so you have not to pay VAT on them. You tell the broker how much you want to spend – probably a minimum of about £3000 – the broker gives you a certificate of size and grading, and informs you every so often how much your diamonds are now worth. When you want to sell, the company has to find someone willing to buy your diamond. This may take time, and you may have difficulty in selling elsewhere if the company cannot find a buyer at a price that suits you. Clearly, the integrity and solvency of the diamond broker are all-important. There is no reason why you should not buy investment diamonds, pay VAT on them, and have them stored and insured here, but this is less profitable.

Diamond funds. There have been offshore diamond bond schemes, through which you invest in a fund which puts some of the money into investment diamonds, while the rest is used to buy gilt-edged investments or placed on deposit. These have done very badly in recent years.

You can also invest in authorised trusts which have an interest in diamond-producing companies, or you could buy shares in De Beers itself.

Other precious stones. All the comments about diamonds apply to other gems, with the further hazard, as the *Financial Times* has warned its readers, of buying 'bargain' stones privately. Even if you know something about stones, the high quality of some synthetic stones makes them very difficult to distinguish from the real thing.

There is no equivalent to the investment diamond trade, so in fact you are buying stones whose main use is for jewellery. If you happen to like them, it's a good time to buy when the market is depressed. The best place to buy is at an auction run by a reputable house, such as Christie's or Phillips in London, as prices tend to be much lower than from dealers.

Currency

When there are no exchange controls, it becomes possible to hold foreign currency as an investment, and fluctuations in the world's exchange rates mean that speculators can make (or lose) large sums of money.

Physicals. All you have to do is open a foreign currency account with one of the High Street banks or a foreign bank with branches in this country. This works in exactly the same way as an ordinary bank account. You get no interest on a current account, but hope to make gains if the exchange rate changes in your favour. Or you can have a deposit account, where you get interest on your investment, as well as the chance of capital gains if the exchange rate moves the right way.

> *Example*
> You buy US dollars when the dollar/sterling exchange rate falls as you get more dollars for your pound. You stash them in your dollar account, and get about 11 per cent interest on them if you want to be able to withdraw them at short notice. When the dollar recovers, and the German mark drops, you sell your dollars and buy marks.

There is usually a minimum deposit of about £1000, and the rates of interest will vary according to how likely that particular currency is to change in the near future, or whether it is generally regarded as unstable. In January 1986, for Swiss francs you could get a rate between 3⅞ and 4⅛ per cent on deposits to be withdrawn at seven days' notice, 4 to 4⅛ per cent for withdrawal at three months' notice. This compared with 8 to 8⅛ per cent on Canadian dollars at seven days' notice, 10 to 10¼ per cent at three months. It pays to shop around both in currencies and in places to deposit your money. At that time you could get 12¼ to 12½ per cent for seven-day sterling bank deposits.

London International Financial Futures Exchange
The latest venture in the City financial markets is LIFFE – the London International Financial Futures Exchange – which opened

on 30 September 1982. This offers a chance to speculate in financial futures contracts in very much the same way as you can on the commodity futures market (see p. 120).

You can take out a futures contract based on different currencies and interest rates, committing you to buy or sell at a fixed price on a fixed date. You have to put up only a proportion of the cost when you take out the contract and you hope to make a profit by anticipating market rates more accurately than the competition. Big money is involved here, but it is hoped that small investors will take up currency contracts, as the maximum for these has been set at £25,000 and only a proportion of this, plus the broker's commission, would have to be put up when taking out the contract. The market is conducted on an 'open outcry' basis, with dealers standing at their pitches shouting the odds, and to make things even more difficult, the prices are quoted in US dollars, as the Chicago Financial Futures Market is the world leader in this field.

The LIFFE trading centre is in the Royal Exchange Building, London EC3.

Currency funds. Because of tax complications most of these are offshore trusts, but those managed by established British companies should be reasonably safe.

Managed currency funds are run on the same principles as unit trusts. You buy units in a fund which buys and sells currencies according to the judgement of the investment managers, who may be presumed to be expert in the highly competitive world of currency markets. The minimum investment ranges from around £500 to £10,000. Charges are about 5 per cent on buying into the fund and 1 per cent per year management charges. You may be able to invest in one of these funds on a regular payments basis, with a minimum payment of about £20 a month.

Currency deposit funds. These are a cross between investing in the managed funds and operating your own deposit account. There are several offshore funds available to UK investors.

One advantage of these funds is that you get interest at deposit rates on the currency you hold added to your stake, as well as any increases in the capital value from dealings in the currencies. You can normally switch your investment from one currency to another at no extra cost.

The best known company in this field is Rothschild's Old Court Fund, based in Jersey, which makes no initial charge and deducts

0.75 per cent a year management charges on the total investment. The minimum investment is the price of one share, approximately £10-£40 each. The other currency deposit funds charge in the same way as the managed funds and require larger minimum deposits. There are no dividends: all the income is re-invested in the funds.

Antiques and collectables

To be a success as an investor in antiques and objets d'art you have to know what you are about. There is no substitute for a personal interest in whatever field you choose, whether it is Persian rugs, early English watercolours, Roman coins, art nouveau pottery, or first editions of modern novelists. If you buy into one of the well-established areas such as Georgian silver or Chippendale, it's unlikely that your investment will increase dramatically in price, although it should maintain its value and keep pace with inflation, allowing for costs. The secret of making a big killing is to spot some untapped source, or unfashionable area, and specialise while prices are still low. Then you have the enjoyment of a fascinating hobby and the chance of becoming an expert in your own right, as well as the possibility of a successful investment.

There are dealers who will do the hard work by recommending how you should invest, or managing a 'portfolio' of collectables for you. You can subscribe so much a month to some of these schemes, and build up your investment gradually. But you are then very dependent on the skill of the dealer, and if there are any bargains to be found, he will get the benefit of them rather than you.

Whether you invest through a dealer or on your own account, you must make sure that what you buy is in perfect condition, and you must keep it that way. Collectors may be interested in items that are less than perfect, but they will never command the best prices, and you cannot be sure that they will maintain their value.

Dealers can sometimes arrange to store items for about 1 per cent of the value annually.

If you are going into antiques for the first time, don't be in too much of a hurry. Investigate the field carefully before you begin (through magazines, dealers' lists, auction reports etc) and buy cheap pieces to begin with. Check up on prices before you pay out any money, as they vary from dealer to dealer. The experts tell you to pick an area of interest which is popular among collectors, as that keeps prices stable. If you are investing in stamps, for instance, it pays to specialise in a part of the world where there is likely to be, now or in the future, an informed collectorship. Don't put too much faith in guaranteed values. One dealer's guarantee may be another's worthless piece of paper. In the end, buy what you like at a price you can afford, and you will be unlucky to lose.

Limited editions. You have seen them in the Sunday colour supplements – 'superbly handcrafted limited editions' of imitation Dresden shepherdesses, or commemorative items. Antiques of the future, they are sometimes called. You have to remember that this kind of object relies largely on scarcity value to maintain a high price. If 5000 or even 500 sets are sold to Sunday paper readers, the editions are not limited enough, as you would find out if you tried to sell them. *Money Which?* tells a sad story of how they made money out of a set of hallmarked silver ingots commemorating 1000 years of British royalty, each with an engraving of one of the rulers. They bought them for £400 six years after they were issued at £350, and sold for £668 six weeks later. But, alas, the reason was a sharp rise in the price of silver. This profitable deal was offered by one who wanted the silver for melting down, not the craftsmanship, so bars of silver would have been a better bet.

Property

Property is the traditional hedge against inflation, because price rises in both private and business property have kept pace with, or done better than inflation for many years, apart from the boom and bust period in commercial property in the early seventies. Don't forget though, that costs such as insurance, rates, and especially repairs and maintenance, have risen too, and that you have to take these into account when judging the value of your investment.

Physicals. You can buy property for yourself to live in or for others to rent. The biggest and best bargain is buying your own home. This is because you get tax relief on the interest you pay on a mortgage loan, up to a maximum mortgage of £30,000. The higher the rate of tax you pay, the better bargain this is. Then when you sell your main home, you do not have to pay capital gains tax on any profit you make, unless you let part of it to someone else, or use it for a business. This means that you can cash in on any increase in value in the price of your house by selling it and buying a more expensive one. With a new mortgage under £30,000 you will continue to get the tax relief on the interest. *Trading up* like this means that you are increasing the value of your investment at little cost. Before you take out a mortgage get some professional advice, as higher rate taxpayers may be better off with an insurance-linked endowment mortgage which costs more but pays a lump sum at the end in addition to the repayment of the loan. A pension mortgage, based on loanback (see p. 111) is another alternative.

Second home. You do not get tax relief on mortgages taken out to buy a second home, unless an elderly dependent relative is to live there rent free, and even then the £30,000 limit on all your mortgages still applies. You may have to pay capital gains tax when you sell, (see p. 162). There will, of course, be extra running costs. Insurance may cost more if the house is empty a lot of the time, but allowing for this, and for capital gains tax, buying a second home as an investment has kept pace with inflation in the past, and you can of course enjoy weekending there.

Holiday letting. If you let your second home for holidays, or buy property especially for holiday letting, you can charge your running costs against the rent you get. Holiday lettings are exempted from the protection given to tenants by the Rent Acts, so there is no problem about that.

Letting to private tenants. This is not worth doing, except perhaps in some luxury areas, because of the difficulties that can be caused by the Rent Acts and the high cost of keeping property in good repair.

Commercial letting. This may be less of a problem than letting to private tenants, but you need to understand the commercial property market, and have a fairly wide spread of different types of property. The high rate of business failures in a period of depression adds to the risks. A new development in this area is in providing small workshops for new businesses. The government is very anxious to help small business revitalise the British economy, so it has devised a small workshop scheme through which you can get tax allowances of 100 per cent of the building cost (excluding land costs) of small workshop or 'nursery' units. This does not have to be new building; many of these projects involve the conversion of a large factory or warehouse into smaller units, with central facilities such as reception and office services. You can let these units to small firms – designers, repairers, craftsmen, printers etc. The scheme was extended in the Finance Act, 1982 until at least 1985, and the maximum size of a single unit qualifying for the full allowance is 2500 square feet. If you want to invest in commercial property to let, this is a good way to begin, as the government subsidy reduces the original cost of your investment by at least the basic rate of tax, and more for higher rate tax-payers.

Funds. The most popular property investment of this kind are property bonds, often linked to life insurance (see p. 96). Investing in a property bond gives you a share in a range of good properties that would otherwise be far out of reach of most private investors. You can draw an income from the fund, and can usually cash in very easily, except at panic times like the property slump of 1974/5. If you decide on a property bond, choose one managed by a company that allows you to switch your investment to another fund, as an extra protection.

You could also invest in unit trusts, investment trusts or directly in shares in property companies.

Home income plans are a way of enabling elderly people to buy an annuity providing them with extra income, using their own home as the security. An insurance company offers a loan of up to 80 per cent of the value of the house, which must normally be worth at least £13,500. This is used to buy an annuity (see p. 108). Part of the income from the annuity goes to pay the interest on the loan. Because this is in fact a mortgage, the interest payments can be set against income tax. Or, if the home owner does not pay tax, the loan can be an option mortgage at a lower interest rate. The rest of the annuity income goes to the home owner. The house remains the property of the home owner, who can benefit from any increase in its value as time goes by. The loan is not repaid until the home owner dies, unless the house is sold before then. In that case, the loan is repaid to the insurance company from the proceeds of the sale, and the annuity continues. As there are no longer any interest payments it is worth more.

Home income plans can be very helpful to people over 70 with small incomes whose main assets are their homes, but who cannot really afford to go on living in them.

Taxing income from property. If you let your second home or holiday home, the Inland Revenue will regard the income as earned income, and tax it accordingly, as long as you follow some basic rules. You must let the place at a commercial rent, must offer it to rent for at least 20 weeks a year, and it must be let for at least 10 weeks. It must be furnished, however simply, and you must not let any tenant stay for more than 31 days during seven months of the year. (You can then allow longer lets during the winter.)

If the Inland Revenue are satisfied, you can charge all expenses from letting, including interest and can deduct personal pension plan contributions.

If you make a loss every year, the Inland Revenue may refuse to allow the trading loss because you are not considered to be trading seriously.

You may be liable to capital gains tax when you sell the property, unless you sell on retirement.

Home income plans are taxed as for other annuities – the payments are regarded as part repayment of capital which is not taxed, and part income, which is assessable for income tax, age income relief and investment income surcharge.

Woodlands

Because the government wants to encourage home-grown wood to reduce imports, there are generous grants and income tax reliefs towards the production of timber. These apply to clearing ground, planting trees and cutting them down. Moreover, there is no capital gains tax when standing timber from a commercial woodland is sold and there are special concessions for capital transfer tax. Then there is the bonus that the land on which the trees grow may also increase in value, though you would be assessed for capital gains tax on any profits on the land when you sell. So woodlands are a very tax-efficient investment, especially in the long term.

Most people cannot afford or do not have the expertise to grow their own, but you can take a share in a forestry trust. The schemes are a kind of syndicate or co-ownership plan – you have a share in woodlands, and in trees which will have matured when the time comes to withdraw your money.

For example, you could buy a £1000 share in a trust designed to produce capital growth with large tax-free distributions in about 25 years' time. The trust would own, say, 200 acres of woodland, planted to produce high yields of commercial pine. After buying the share for £1000, you might be asked to pay 7.5 per cent charges for the next two years, and about 2 per cent annually after that – these charges would be income tax deductible. Depending on inflation and timber prices, the shares would be expected to increase about fourfold – in other words, you would get back four times as much as you paid in, allowing for inflation. If you wanted to sell out before the scheme matured, the trust would hope to find a buyer for your share, at a price that took into account the increase in the capital value while you had owned it. Fountain Forestry have produced a free booklet *Forestry Facts* which sets out the rules about tax incentives for investing in woodland. It is available from Fountain Forestry Ltd, 35 Queen Anne Street, London W1M 9FB; tel: 01-631 0845.

The recession has affected timber prices as much as everything else, but trees are nothing if not a long-term investment; you must plan in advance when you want your investment to mature. It may be difficult to cash in early. Under existing schemes, you do not expect to get a regular income from woodlands; the attraction is capital growth while minimising capital gains and capital transfer taxes. There are other risks involved besides fluctuations in the price of timber. Woods can be insured against many risks but not disease. This is a good reason for joining a group scheme which can to some extent spread the risk over different types of tree and different areas.

Small businesses

Many people dream of owning a corner newsagent's, or a teashop serving home-made scones with jam and Devonshire cream, but this is not the place to discuss whether that is the way to make a good living. It would be impossible to do justice here to all the different ways of setting up on your own. We are concerned with putting your money into *someone else's* business, sitting back, and receiving some of the profits in return for the use of your nest egg. *Franchising* is neither one thing nor the other. You put your money into someone else's company, but you have to run the business yourself. So we are not considering that either.

However, there are plenty of opportunities for the venturesome investor. Governments are all in favour of small businesses, and offer incentives in the form of tax reliefs and grants to help them grow and develop. These are an incentive to the investor too;

the risks of putting your money into a new and untried business are less daunting if you are getting tax reliefs which reduce the cost to you. And quite apart from the tax reliefs to investors, the other grants and concessions ought to make it much easier for the nouveau entrepreneur to make a profit. In enterprise zones, for example, companies get full exemption from rates for 10 years, 100 per cent tax allowances on buildings, less red tape, and plenty of other support and good advice. It should be easy to do well, but it is still a risky business. Investors in Industry (previously Finance for Industry) which lends more to small business than most other financial institutions, reckons that about one in three new companies fails in the early years. On the other hand, this might be your chance to get in at the beginning of some new technology or a new service that will one day expand into a multi-million-pound business.

There are two main ways of investing privately in a company: you can make a *loan* to the firm, which is paid back by instalments, together with interest. You should make sure that this is *secured* on some of the firm's assets, eg a mortgage on the building; otherwise, if the firm does go bankrupt, you will be in no better position than any other unsecured creditor and may get very little of your money back. (The firm may not be able to offer you any security on a loan if it has already borrowed from other sources such as the bank.) Or you can buy a share in the firm's *equity*. In other words you become a part-owner of the firm, and you share the profits, if any, that the business makes. Your stake is limited to the number of shares you buy, so although you could lose your investment if the firm went bankrupt, you would not be liable for any more debts it might have run up. Equity financing is more risky than a secured loan, but if the firm does very well, you will get a greater share of the profits, and should be able to sell out your stake at a profit as well.

It goes without saying that you should find out as much as possible about a firm before lending it money, even if the owner is one of your oldest friends. You should ask to see estimated profit and loss accounts, balance sheets, and audited accounts for previous years, if possible. Make sure the firm has a carefully thought out plan for using the money and that the business can support the extra costs, especially in the short term. It would be worth getting advice from your bank manager or accountant about setting up this kind of deal.

If you are interested in putting money into a small business, but don't know of any which are looking for capital, your bank manager, accountant, solicitor, or stockbroker may be able to suggest one. Many local chambers of commerce run an advisory service for small firms, and would be able to suggest likely candidates. The London Enterprise Agency, for example, runs what it calls a marriage bureau. This can put potential investors in touch with firms who need backing. You can contact the bureau at LEntA, 69 Cannon Street, London EC4N 5AB; tel: 01-236 2676. Each month the agency issues a bulletin in which subscribers can advertise anonymously. Anyone interested can reply to the advertisement through the box number given, and the agency can arrange an introduction if this seems appropriate. For £12 you get a six months' subscription to the bulletin, and can put in one advertisement, drafted with the help of the agency staff.

Examples from one issue include:

Partner for microcomputer venture
Businessman with up to £20,000 to invest wishes to meet person interested in starting microcomputer business in its various aspects including a retail outlet. Location NW London. Other person should preferably have experience in computer field and some capital to invest.

Venture capital require
Newly established company formed to handle sole UK marketing and distribution of a luxury replica motor sports vehicle, new to the UK market, requires £100,000 capital, split in units of £10,000. Sole distributorship may be extended to Europe and Middle East. The project is planned as a viable business.

Equity offered for £30,000, participation possible
Young company producing a new form of printing outfit seeks investment of £30,000. The product has enormous potential in the educational, stationery and toy markets. It is patented in the UK, USA, Canada, France and W. Germany, and has been selected by the Design Centre, London. Participation also possible for the right person with marketing skills.

Business Expansion Scheme
The BES has been eagerly seized upon by companies seeking to make the most of the generous tax concessions it offers.

At present, investors get tax concessions on investment in any company just starting up, or engaged mainly in trade which is not quoted on the stock market, or the Unlisted Securities Market. They can claim an investment of up to £40,000 maximum in any one year against their highest rates of tax.

There are conditions to be satisfied. The investment must be in new shares or additional capital. Shares must be kept for five years; if you sell before the five years is up you lose the tax relief.

You must be an *outsider* – you must not own more than 30 per cent of the total shares, and you must not be an active director, employee or partner in the firm. Nor must your business partners or spouse, parents, grandparents, children, take any active part in the firm. There is a minimum of £500 investment per company.

There is the usual risk of losing your money as for any investment in a new venture, and you also need to be aware of the rule that if the company ceases to qualify for the scheme within three years, or ceases trading, you can lose all the tax relief you have claimed, and may have to repay the Inland Revenue.

There are investment funds, much advertised in the press, especially just before the end of the tax year, which collect funds from a number of would-be investors, and invest these in a number of qualifying firms, so that the risks are spread. If these funds are approved by the Inland Revenue, the £500 minimum does not apply.

BES is a risky investment, in whatever form it takes, but the rewards of investing in a successful new venture can be correspondingly high.

Interest relief scheme

If you borrow money to invest in a *close company*, that is a company where five people or fewer own more than half the shares, you can get tax relief on the interest you pay. You have to meet one of two conditions to qualify for this. You must either own more than 5 per cent of the shares, or you must be a shareholder and work for the business most of your time.

Example
You borrow £5000 from the bank to buy shares in your brother's car repair firm, at an interest rate of 12 per cent. You can set this interest – £600 – against tax, so if you are paying at the basic rate it actually costs you £400. He would have to pay you a dividend of more than 8 per cent, tax paid, to make it worth your while.

Venture capital scheme

If you invest money in a company not quoted on the Stock Exchange, an *unquoted trading company*, and you lose money when you sell the shares, you may be able to set this loss against your income, as a deduction for income tax assessment. You or your spouse must be the original owner of the shares, ie you must have bought them from the company when they were first issued, not from a previous shareholder. This is because the scheme is intended to encourage people to put *new* money into small businesses. It would apply to a firm selling its shares on the Unlisted Securities Market for the first time, or making an issue of new shares there, so it is an extra incentive to deal in the market (see p. 65).

The scheme is useful if you would like to help a small company, but don't pay capital gains tax and therefore are not able to set any losses against other gains. It gives you some chance of reducing the amount you lose if the company is unsuccessful, as you at least get a tax rebate.

Capital transfer tax
If you hold shares in an unquoted company for more than two years, you can claim relief of capital transfer tax if you give the shares away: 20 per cent of the tax due.

The IG Index

The small investor can speculate on gold and other commodity prices without having to lay out large sums of money and without paying income or capital gains tax. The secret is in a superior kind of betting shop. Instead of buying contracts for futures you make bets on what the prices are going to be and because this is a form of gambling, the operators pay betting duty instead of other taxes, and the punters pay no tax at all. The IG (Investors' Gold) Index began by taking bets on gold prices, and now offers bets on all the major commodity futures traded in London, New York and Chicago, from aluminium to frozen pork bellies. You can also bet on the movements in share indices, currencies and interest rates.

In the last 18 months there has been an enormous growth in betting on traded options on most of these futures. IG have even created their own traded options on the Financial Times Industrial Ordinary Share Index and on the Dow Jones Index (which measures prices on the New York Stock Exchange).

To bet with IG Index you have first to be accepted as an account holder. You can then make bets by telephone at any time in business hours (8.30 am to 9.00 pm).

You can bet that prices on any index will go up or down. When you bet, IG Index will quote you a higher and a lower price from which the rise or fall is calculated. The spread between these 'buying' and 'selling' prices is where IG Index makes its profits and covers its expenses and betting tax; there are no other charges. You name the index you want to bet on, and the amount per point you want to bet that it will go *up* or *down*.

You might choose to bet that the price of gold will go up in the next three months, ie that the price in dollars per ounce will rise. If you bet £10 a point – the points represent the units in which that particular currency or commodity is usually quoted – and gold goes up by $40 an ounce you have won 10 × 40 = £400, tax-free.

When the bet is confirmed you will be given a date on which the bet will automatically be closed, but you can close it at any time you choose before then. When you make the bet you have to pay a deposit of between 5 and 15 per cent of the value of the bet ie 5-15 per cent of the starting price multiplied by the amount per point you want to bet. So if the gold price was $400 when you took out the bet at £10 a point, your deposit would be 15 per cent of £4000 ie £600. You do not receive any interest on the deposits or money held in your account. If the price changes dramatically against you, you may be asked to decide either to increase your deposit or to close the bet, before you lose too much money. There are different minimum bets per point for the different indices.

Two examples, quoted by IG Index:

A down bet in coffee
The client calls on 20 August and asks for our quotation for March coffee. We quote 2560 to 2573 per tonne. The client expects the price to fall, and he makes an £8 down bet at 2560. The deposit required was £3000, ie approximately 15 per cent of the value of 8 tonnes of coffee. On 14 November the client calls and finds that our quotation for March coffee is 2300 to 2314. He closes his bet at 2314. His profit is calculated as follows:

Opening level	2560
Closing level	2314
Difference	246

Profit on an £8 down bet: 246 × £8 = £1968, tax-free.

He also, of course, receives back his £3000 deposit.

An up bet on the Dow Jones Index
On 27 March, the client calls and asks our quotation on the June Dow Jones Index. We quote 1681 to 1689. The client expects the price to rise, and he makes a £30 up bet at 1689. He will make £30 for every point by which his closing level is above 1689, (deposit 1689 × 30 × 5 per cent = £2500). He will lose £30 for every point by which his closing level is below 1689. On 3 May he asks for the June Dow Jones Index price again. Our

quotation is 1969 to 1975. He decides to close his bet, and so it is closed at 1969. His profit is calculated as follows:

Closing level	1969
Opening level	1689
Difference	280

Profit on a £30 up bet: 280 × £30 = £8,400, free of tax, plus deposit.

Full details from IG Index Ltd, 9-11 Grosvenor Gardens, London SW1W 0BD, tel: 01-828 7233.

Other bookmaking chains offer this kind of betting on a more limited scale.

Summary

SAFETY

Will the capital be repaid in full?	Not necessarily.
Are the investments officially regulated?	No.
Is the capital protected against inflation?	Possibly in the long term.

AVAILABILITY	Fair.

METHOD

How do you invest?	Through broker, dealer, or direct.
Are there commission charges?	Yes, for brokers and dealers.
Are there extra charges when you buy and sell?	Possibly.

INCOME

Is income paid regularly?	No, except trusts.
Is it guaranteed?	No.
Are there prospects for capital gains?	Yes.
Is the income high/average/low?	Depends.

TAXATION

Is the return assessed for income tax?	Varies.

Is basic rate deducted?	No.
Can the tax be reclaimed?	—
Is it assessed for age income relief?	Possibly.
Is it assessed for capital gains tax?	Usually.

Chapter 9

Special Cases

.

Investing abroad

When there are no exchange controls, people in this country can invest anywhere in the world they like and since exchange controls were fully lifted in 1979 the big institutions, for instance, have taken full advantage of the opportunity. Income from investments in overseas companies is now a major contributor to the credit side of the balance of payments. But, and this is a fairly large but, if exchange controls are reintroduced, as a future government might well decide to do, investment abroad could run into considerable difficulties. At present (February 1986), there is no doubt that by investing abroad you can spread the risks and increase your chances of getting a high return, provided you take care and obtain the most reliable information before you commit yourself.

How safe is your money?
The risks of investing abroad are very much the same as those for different kinds of investment at home, with the extra hazards of not knowing the language, the local conditions, and the local rules. Strangers often rush in where locals fear to tread.

There are also the extra uncertainties involved in operating in a different currency from your own. If the exchange rate alters, your profits could be wiped out when you bring them home, or you could get an extra bonus you hadn't expected. Suppose you had bought a cottage in France which cost the equivalent of £5000 in the days when the franc was about 8 to the pound sterling, ie 40,000 francs. If you sold it for what you paid for it when the franc had dropped to 12 francs to the pound, you would take home $40,000 \div 12 = F3,333$, a loss of about 33 per cent. Suppose you had bought your cottage in Florida for the equivalent of £5000 when the dollar was down to 2.40 to the pound, ie 12,000 dollars. If you sold for the same price when the dollar had recovered to 1.40 to the pound, you would have received $12,000 \div 1.40 = £8571$, a profit of 90 per cent.

When the pound goes up, the return from your investments abroad goes down; when the pound falls, you get more for your money if you bring it home. That's one reason why investments abroad are attractive in hard times at home. The trick is to *buy* the investment when the pound is strong so it costs you less in real terms, and *sell* when the pound falls, so you get more pounds back.

Are there any limits on investment?
At present there are no limits on the British side, but you need to know about local regulations that may affect your investments. If, for example, you open a bank account in a foreign country, you may find that you cannot necessarily withdraw the money and take it home. If you buy property in some countries, you may be regarded as a resident, subject to local taxes and exchange controls.

How do you invest?
In some cases you can invest through your stockbroker or bank in the usual way, otherwise you will often need a trustworthy and efficient agent in the foreign country, who may be hard to find.

What return does it provide?
This depends on the type of investment, but unless the return is higher than you would expect to get at home, you should have compelling reasons for investing abroad – perhaps because you hope to retire there, or run a business there, or don't mind speculating with extra risks in the hope of extra profits.

How is it taxed?
It doesn't matter where you make your money – the Inland Revenue will still want to tax it. So any income from overseas investment, even if you leave it abroad, must be declared to the Inland Revenue, and any capital gains (or losses) you make are assessed for capital gains tax. Capital transfer tax still applies to gifts you make to friends or relatives abroad of property and other assets you own in a foreign country.

Some income and capital gains will also be subject to local taxes before you can bring the money home. In most cases you will be entitled to some tax concessions, because the British government has double taxation agreements with many foreign countries. The tax burden is shared between the two governments so you do not have to pay twice on the same money. You can get full details from your local Inland Revenue office. Sometimes interest and dividends will be paid to you with the local tax due already deducted in full, and you will have to apply for the double taxation concession yourself. Again, the Inland Revenue can help you.

If the foreign government deducts its share of tax (usually at a rate of 15 per cent) under a double taxation agreement, and under British tax rules you would not be paying tax, you can't claim a refund from the British tax office and are unlikely to get anything back from the foreign authorities.

This all supposes that you remain a resident of Great Britain. If you decide to live abroad for most of the year, different rules apply. You would need an accountant to sort this out for you.

What types of investment are there?

Most of the investments discussed in Part One are available in foreign countries. Here are some of the main points to bear in mind when considering whether to invest in them abroad:

Stocks and shares

Government stocks. Foreign governments raise money in the same way as our own government does, through gilt-edged securities. You can buy and sell some of these loans on the London Stock Exchange, and your stockbroker or bank can also deal in stocks on foreign exchanges. He will be able to carry out the necessary formalities for you, buy currency, obtain certificates etc. The cost will be a bit higher than for home dealings. Gains and losses made from the sale of foreign stocks are assessed for capital gains tax, unlike British government stocks.

Shares in foreign companies. Similarly, your stockbroker or bank can deal for you in shares in foreign companies quoted on the London Exchange, or on foreign exchanges. It's more risky, because you are at some disadvantage in keeping abreast of what's going on in foreign stock markets, and because the official supervision of the affairs of foreign businesses may be less stringent than our own. You may need to invest £10,000-£15,000 to make it worthwhile, and to get a good spread of risks and opportunities.

143

Unit and investment trusts. There are authorised British unit trusts and investment trusts who specialise in foreign companies and these are probably the best bet for small investors who want to include some foreign investment in their portfolio. At least you have the standard protection available to investors in British firms.

Offshore trusts and foreign banks. Because these are based abroad, often in *tax havens* – countries whose taxes are much lower than ours – they can offer higher returns than many British trusts, and can also offer funds investing in commodities or currency which British authorised trusts are not permitted to do.

However, this is a very speculative area, and you can get your fingers badly burned. There have been several major scandals which at least have had the effect of persuading foreign governments to take a more interventionist line into the financial affairs of companies operating in their area. Although these firms are allowed to advertise in this country, the investments are not covered by British company law or the official agencies which protect investors against loss, such as the Policy-Holders' Protection Board.

There are offshore funds run by subsidiaries of large, well-known financial groups, so if you do want to invest in an offshore fund it's best to choose one with a well-known British or international company behind it.

Eurobonds. When an institution borrows money on the international money market in a currency which is not that of its home country, it is dealing in *Eurocurrency*. There's not necessarily any connection with Europe in the deal; it could be a South African firm borrowing American dollars. *Eurobonds* are bonds by which institutions can raise money on the Eurocurrency market. The minimum investment is high, perhaps $10,000, and it may be expensive to buy or sell small amounts.

Although Eurobonds are quoted on some of the world's stock exchanges, most Eurobonds are bought and sold through agents such as banks and other financial institutions. Your stockbroker or bank could advise you if you were interested.

Eurobonds are issued for fixed terms, at a fixed rate of interest, though some may offer rates that vary with the market. The return is paid at the end of the term without deduction of tax, and is assessable for income tax and age allowance. Gains and losses made from the sales of the bonds are assessable for capital gains tax. Details of dealings and prices for Eurobonds, and the range of Eurocurrency rates, are published regularly in the financial press.

Property

This is the boom area in investment abroad, as many people would love to own a place in the sun which could double as an investment. The picture may not be quite as rosy as some of the promoters claim. It is essential to deal with a reputable firm. You may find it simpler and more convenient to use an established British firm of estate or travel agents, for example. You ought, if at all possible, to visit the place before you commit yourself in any way. If you are buying a house or flat as an investment to rent out to holiday makers, think about the management costs: who is going to see that the villa is kept in good order and ready for each new tenant? Don't forget that if you want to use it yourself for holidays you have to forgo income if you are tied to school holidays, or want to be there at the peak season of the year. If you are thinking about retirement, the best place to live all the year round may not be the tourist trap holiday centre that is more likely to provide a good income from letting. It is essential to get good professional advice, from a disinterested source, before you buy.

You also need to remember that the standards of the legal profession in some countries may not be as high as they are here. Horror stories about losing all your savings because the same flat has been sold to several different people are unfortunately not uncommon.

Timeshare. If you do not want the hassle and expense of buying a house or flat, you can now buy a share in one. With *timeshare*, or shared ownership, you buy specified weeks in a holiday home abroad (or in this country). This gives you the right to a holiday there for those weeks for a fixed period of time – 10, 20 or more years. A management company looks after the maintenance and repairs. There are agencies that can arrange for you to swop weeks with other owners in other places if you get bored with your own property.

Again, it is essential to deal with a reputable firm, and the activities of some less reputable ones have provoked the formation of the British Property Timeshare Association, a trade association dedicated to raising standards and increasing the popularity of timeshare. Although it is not designed at present to act as a referee for dissatisfied customers, it has produced helpful guidelines for would-be purchasers which anyone contemplating buying overseas property would do well to consider, obtainable free from the Secretary, BPTA, Westminster Bank Chambers, Market Hill, Sudbury, Suffolk CO10 6EN; tel: 0787 313 424.

Points to watch

● You have to keep an eye on international politics as well as international finance.
● Don't take any information at its face value, check it out. For instance, some offshore trusts are not above giving their company a name very similar to one of the famous banking names to provide themselves with extra (spurious) status.
● Try and talk to a native of the country, or someone who knows it well before you take your decision.
● The Inland Revenue has a way of catching up with those who don't tell the whole truth, even when the assets disregarded are in another country. The penalties for tax evasion are severe.
● Don't assume that rules and customs abroad are the same as for British financial institutions and transactions. There may be quite important differences.

Investing for children

If you are under 18, you can own most of the investments discussed in this book in your own right, and those you cannot own can be held in trust for you. The main legal limitation on ownership of investments for people under 18 is that they cannot own real property, that is, land and buildings. Other limitations may be imposed by the various institutions offering investments, especially in view of the fact that people under 18 cannot be held legally responsible if they fail to keep their side of some contracts. But there is no objection in law to young people owning investments in building societies, banks, unit trusts etc.

The rules are different for people who marry before they are 18.

There is also a distinction to be made between assets that belong to the individual child, and assets that are held in trust. If the money or other asset was given to or earned by the child, it belongs to that child, and he or she can make what they like of it without reference to anyone, other than the natural moral authority of a parent or guardian. So in theory, children can cash it in, spend it or transfer it to some other investment off their own bat, without anyone else's permission.

If the investment is held in trust for a child, the trustees have to administer the trust on behalf of the beneficiaries and they may have the discretion, depending on the type of trust, to decide how this should be done and what the money should be spent on. A trust does not necessarily come to an end when the beneficiary reaches the age of 18; whoever endows the trust can make what conditions, within reason, they choose, eg that no money should be paid out until the beneficiary is 25, gets married, or goes to college.

So if you want to be sure that the money you give your god-children is not spent on a 1000 cc motorbike, or squandered by a wicked stepfather, you may prefer to put the money in trust or into a long-term investment that is difficult to cash in early, rather than giving it to them outright.

If you do decide to set up a trust, the effects of taxation and the difficulties in getting the result you intend make it advisable to get professional help from a solicitor.

Taxation

The tax inspector discourages parents from making investments for their children, because any income received by children under 18 from investments paid for by their parents is added to the *parents'* taxable income apart from the first £5, which is tax free – a princely concession.

Otherwise, children under 18 are liable for income tax and investment income surcharge in the normal way. It is important to note that they receive the same tax allowances and concessions that an adult is entitled to. So a child can receive earned or investment income up to the level of the personal allowance (£2335 in 1986-7) before having to pay tax, as long as the investment did not originate from the parents. This means that grandparents, other relatives, friends etc can make gifts to children without their parents having to pay extra tax. As most children will not be paying income tax, there is no advantage in choosing tax-free or tax-paid investments for them, especially if the tax paid cannot be re-claimed.

As far as capital gains tax or inheritance tax is concerned, this is assessed in the usual way. Gifts to or from children are assessable for both taxes, including gifts from parents to children. If a child makes a capital gain on an investment, this is *not* added to the parents' total when any tax due is calculated. So if a parent wants to make a gift to a child, it may be an advantage to choose the kind of investment that aims at capital growth rather than providing an income.

The tax advantages of covenants are particularly good when investing for children, as they are unlikely to have to pay any tax and get the full benefit from the money covenanted. (See p. 167.)

What types of investment are there?

The financial institutions have their own rules about investment by people under 18 so find out what these are before choosing. Some of the main points to note about the investments discussed in Part One are as follows:

National Savings. All the National Savings investments except SAYE can be bought for children from birth, but until the children are seven years old, the investments may not be cashed in.

Building societies. The rules vary according to the society. There is often a minimum age of seven, and some special children's saver accounts may not be cashed in until the child is 18.

High Street banks. You can have a deposit account from birth, but have to be able to write a signature in order to take money out. Trustee Savings Banks may not allow any withdrawals before the child is seven.

Gilt-edged securities. These can be bought through the National Savings Stock Register for or by people under 18, but may not be sold by children under seven.

Stocks and shares. Although you can own these under 18, it may be difficult to deal in them except with the help of an adult nominee.

Unit trusts. The rules vary according to the trust. M & G, for example, will allow units to be held for children in designated accounts, which can be transferred into the child's name at 14 or over; children over 14 can buy and sell units.

Life insurance. Some insurance companies will not offer policies for people under 18, so you would need to check with a broker about the best firms to approach.

Pensions schemes. It's expecting rather a lot to interest young people in a pension plan, and in any case to get full benefit of the tax concessions, they would have to have qualifying earnings from some kind of self-employment to make it worthwhile.

Investing in things. Because the main object of this kind of investment is to increase the value of capital, it may be quite a good buy for young people under 18. There's always a good chance that today's 'bygone' may be tomorrow's antique, and there is the extra satisfaction of appreciating the beauty of the object while it appreciates in value. The more speculative forms of investment in currency or commodities would be neither suitable or practicable!

If you have any problems about the law and investment for children, the Children's Legal Centre, 20-21 Compton Terrace, London N1 2UN may be able to help. (Please enclose a stamped-addressed envelope with your query.)

Points to watch

- Don't tie up money in a trust so tightly that it can't be used sensibly in an emergency or unforeseen event.
- It costs money to set up a trust and have it properly administered. A term investment may serve the same purpose at less cost.
- Don't overlook the possibility of reclaiming tax deducted at source from children's income.
- Remember that when a child becomes a student any income received from investments will be taken into account when the student grant is calculated.
- If you want to make gifts for investment by your own children it makes sense to go for capital growth and tax-free choices such as National Savings Certificates, so as to reduce the tax bill.
- When making a present to someone else's child, the easy way out is to hand over £25 each Christmas and leave it at that. But with a little thought you could, for example, covenant the £25, so that the child can claim the tax relief of 29 per cent, which increases it to £35. Then if the annual payment is invested in a regular savings scheme, and the income from that re-invested, it could easily double in value by the time the seven-year covenant is up, thus providing a useful nest egg.

Investing for people over 65

Everyone will have been telling you for years that you must make retirement plans long before you reach the age of 65, but whatever advance planning you have done, retirement is the time to look very carefully at all your investments, income and outgoings, to ensure that you are making the best use of your resources and any tax concessions available. There's plenty of good advice around, so make the most of it.

Taxation

Unfortunately, pensions are subject to tax like any other income, whether from the state, your employer or from a personal plan. They are not subject to investment income surcharge, as long as what you paid for them did not exceed the permitted tax concession limits.

Don't forget the *earnings rule* which reduces the amount of state pension you get if you earn more than about £70 a week. So if you continue working, it may be worth delaying the receipt of your state pension, which you can do up to age 70, and this will increase its value slightly. The earnings rule does *not* apply to income from investments or other pensions.

The problem for people on a moderate income is the age allowance. As explained under Taxation, (see p. 158) you are entitled to full age allowance from the tax year in which you become 65, as long as your income does not exceed £9400. Age allowance is reduced in stages until you receive just the ordinary personal allowance if your income is about £10,000. So if you are on the margin of this tax threshold, it makes sense to choose investments that are not counted towards your taxable income.

You have to pay capital gains tax in the normal way and, unfortunately, you cannot average out any gains from life insurance policies – any gain you make on a single premium policy is added to the current year's income when the calculation is made for age allowance.

Now is the time to start thinking about how to lessen the effects of inheritance tax if you want to leave as much as you can behind you, and haven't yet made any plans.

The charity Age Concern publishes a useful guide, *Your Taxes and Savings in Retirement*, price £1.50, or £1.70 including postage, from Age Concern, 60 Pitcairn Road, Mitcham, Surrey CR4 3LL; tel: 01-640 5431.

What types of investment are there?

Your choice will depend on whether your income is low enough to escape tax altogether, is on the verge of losing age allowance, or is fully subject to tax. For people over 65, there are a few special points to watch. In particular, a married couple needs to look more carefully at the special provisions that may affect a fixed-term investment if one partner dies before the term is up, and take these into account when making a choice.

National Savings. The tax-free investments are an obvious choice if you pay tax, and if you plan your investments of National Savings Certificates carefully, for instance, you can encash them in a planned sequence without paying tax on the 'income' you receive. The income bonds and investment account offer a high return to non-taxpayers. If you are worried about the effect of inflation on your capital, the lump-sum SAYE schemes may be worth considering.

Banks. Why keep your money in a deposit account at the bank if you could get more without deduction of tax from the National Savings Investment account? Yet this is what a number of pensioners tend to do because it is less trouble.

Building societies. The same applies to building societies, especially if you are not paying tax and so cannot reclaim the tax deducted.

Gilt-edged securities and other loans. These are worth considering as long as you don't need the capital early or in a hurry.

Stocks and shares. Investing in shares may become a worthwhile hobby once you have more time to indulge in it, and keep track of what is happening to your investments. If you can afford to risk some of your capital, you could find a new interest in the traded options market, for example.

Life insurance. The cost of investing in life insurance may rise as you get older, but it has advantages, especially if you want to provide for your family.

Pensions. When you decide what options to take from your pension, you need to consider your tax position and how, for example, having a lump sum invested rather than a larger pension will affect it. Take advantage of the open market option that allows you to shop around for your pension (see p. 107). And you can go on paying into a scheme after 65.

Investing in things. Again this may provide a new interest as well as profit. Don't forget the capital gains tax concession that allows you to dispose of 'chattels' – which could be objets d'art or jewellery – under £3000 in value without paying CGT.

Points to watch

- This is necessarily only a brief guide to points to look out for. Don't leave it till too late to get the best possible advice.
- Don't stint yourself in order to provide for your heirs; you deserve a comfortable retirement.
- Although tax may seem to bear very heavily on retirement income, that's not a reason for settling for a lower return than you could get by changing your investments. The tax man can never take it *all*, so an extra 1 or 2 per cent is worth having.
- If you decide to retire and live abroad, this may affect your entitlement to state pensions and social security. It's best to choose somewhere which has reciprocal agreements with the British government.
- If your income is not enough for your needs, think about raising money on your house as described on p. 131.
- If you want to help an elderly person financially, it's worth covenanting the money, as long as they don't pay tax.
- Enjoy yourself, it's earlier than you think.

Part Two
What you need to know about how the system works

Here you will find some of the basic information about taxes, interest rates and the financial press and other advisers that you'll need to make investment decisions. We look at the taxes that make a difference to how you invest money, what happens to interest rates, the kinds of financial advice you may find helpful, and we explain a few of the words that may puzzle newcomers.

Chapter 10

Taxes and Investment

'It was as true,' said Mr Barkis, 'as taxes is, and nothing's truer than them.'

Charles Dickens, *David Copperfield*

At least, if you take the trouble to find out the rules, you can make taxes work for rather than against you where your investments are concerned.

For a simple, plain man's guide to tax and the individual, you can't do better than the annual tax guide in *Which?* published as a supplement each March with a follow-up on the Budget in June. As it would be quite impossible to cover all the ins and outs of income tax here, not to mention the finer points of capital gains tax and capital transfer tax, this section aims to point you in the right direction by explaining the basic principles of the taxes that are likely to affect your investments. Details about the tax advantages and disadvantages of different types of investment are given in the respective investment section in Part One.

The first and best rule is: when in doubt, ask an expert. This could be an accountant, a specialist tax adviser, or even your friendly neighbourhood tax inspector, who will often give very good advice. Some of the best financial brains in the country spend their time working out yet more ingenious schemes of investment that make the best use of tax concessions. Once you understand the basic principles you can get the benefit of all this expertise simply by keeping an eye on the financial press – the advertisements as well as the news and comment.

The figures given here refer to rates and allowances for the tax year 1986-7. Taxes and allowances vary from year to year, so it is important to make sure you have the latest figures.

Income tax

It makes no difference where your income comes from – salary or wages; profits from self-employment; interest from investments –

it's all taxed in the same way and the basic principles of income tax apply. These are that you get allowances according to your responsibilities and commitments. What's left is your *taxable income* and you pay tax on it according to a scale which starts at the *basic rate* of 29 per cent for the first £17,200.

Scales for 1986-7

Taxable income	Tax rate %
up to £17,200	29
£17,201-£20,200	40
£20,201-£25,400	45
£25,401-£33,300	50
£33,301-£41,200	55
Above £41,200	60

The step from one tax rate to the next is known as a *tax threshold* and if you are on the threshold the extra income you make from an investment may push you up into a higher rate or *tax bracket*. This is one of the points you have to watch when considering the pros and cons of different investments. It could be, for example, that you would be better off with a lower return from a tax-free investment like National Savings Certificates than with higher interest subject to tax.

Any tax-free investments are a better bargain for taxpayers than they are for those whose income is too low to pay income tax, and the higher your tax rate, the more any tax concessions are worth to you, as the amounts are deducted from your highest rate of tax.

Example

Someone who is self-employed and has taxable earnings of £10,000 can put £1750 in a personal pension plan, and get 29 per cent tax relief on the contributions, ie he or she has £507.50 less to pay in tax. Someone who is self-employed and has taxable earnings of £45,000 who puts £1750 in a personal pension plan gets 60 per cent tax relief. He or she has £1050 less to pay to the tax inspector, exactly more than twice as much relief for the same contribution.

Investment income surcharge

This was abolished from the tax year beginning 6 April 1984.

Marriage and investment income

This is one area of taxation where there is no advantage in being married, because the Inland Revenue allots investment income to the husband, regardless of whether he or his wife owns the investment, even if they have chosen to be taxed separately. This has several disadvantages:

● When income from a wife's investments is added to the husband's earnings it may push his tax rate into a higher tax bracket, though if they were taxed separately, the wife would be paying just the basic rate on her interest. So, for example, if a wife puts her savings in a building society, in the belief that any tax due is taken care of by the society, the husband may get a bill for extra tax because the interest from the building society is added to his income and brings it into a higher tax band.

● A single woman can set her single person's allowance against investment income if she has no other earnings, and so reduce her tax bill. A married woman can claim an *earned* income allowance, but not to set against investment income.

A possible new structure for taxing married couples is contained in a recent Green Paper which, if implemented, might remedy some of the present anomalies.

Different ways of paying tax on investments

Not all investment income is taxed, and when tax is due it may be collected in different ways. These differences are important, and will affect your choice of which investment to buy. There are three main kinds of investment as far as taxation is concerned:

Tax-free investments. No tax is payable on income from these, which are mainly government sponsored savings schemes. The income and any increase in the value are not counted when calculations about interest, age allowances, married couple's investment income etc are made. So they are excellent value for taxpayers, especially in the higher tax brackets.

National Savings Bank ordinary accounts offer a special concession in that each individual who holds an account can have the first £70 of interest tax free; not a large amount but it gives a high return for the top rate taxpayer if it's not beneath his contempt.

Tax-paid (tax deducted at source) *investments.* The income from these, eg dividends from stocks and shares, is taxed at the basic rate of 29 per cent before the money is paid to you. So if you are a basic rate taxpayer there is no problem, and nothing extra to pay.

You will receive *tax credits* or *tax deduction certificates* from the institutions paying the dividend for the amount that you are deemed to have paid, and should also receive a *tax voucher* setting out the gross interest you would have received including the tax credited to you, and other details for your records.

If you have to pay a higher rate of tax, the tax inspector will send you a bill for the extra amount due.

To calculate this, the Inland Revenue plays its trick of 'grossing up', ie it works out how much you would have received if an amount equivalent to 29 per cent basic rate tax had been paid to you along with the interest, and then charges the additional tax due on that total. If you don't pay tax at all, you can normally claim a refund of the tax paid on your behalf from the Inland Revenue.

Taxed at composite rate. Building societies, banks and other loans now all deduct tax at the composite rate before paying you the interest due. You can't claim a refund if you normally pay no tax. If your income is high enough, you still have to pay any extra amount due because of the difference between your tax rate and the basic rate.

> *Example*
> Your top rate of tax is 40 per cent and you receive £71 in interest from the building society with tax at the basic rate accounted for. The Inland Revenue would gross that £71 up to £100 to include the notional 29 per cent tax, and then ask you for another £10 to make up the tax bill of £40.

Similar rules apply to some life insurance linked investments that pay a regular income (see p. 97).

Untaxed investments. For these investments, eg a private loan, the income is paid without deductions and you have to pay any tax due. The Inland Revenue normally collects this on a 'preceding year' basis, ie you are charged tax in the current year on the amount you received in interest last year, with special arrangements for the first and last years in which you hold the investment. If the interest you receive from an investment varies a lot from year to year you may be able to reduce the amount of tax payable by using these special rules – ask your accountant as it is quite complicated.

Age allowance
This is an extra personal allowance against income tax given to people who are or will be 65 in the current tax year, whether or not

they have retired. The rates in 1986-7 are £2850 for a single person, and £4505 for a married couple if at least one of the partners is 65.

The allowance is reduced if your total income is over £9400, by £2 for every £3 over that amount, until you are back to the level of the normal personal income tax allowances. Your *total income* is made up of your gross income, including:

Your and your spouse's earned income;
Grossed up taxable investment income;
Income from pensions, including state pensions.

You can deduct from this:

Mortgage payments;
Other interest payments qualifying for tax relief;
Authorised contributions to a personal pension plan;
The gross amount of covenant payments to others.

What's left is your total income. You should always claim age allowance if you qualify, as you cannot be worse off by claiming. You will never get *less* than the ordinary personal allowances.

Points to watch

- Many people pay tax on investment income which they could avoid by putting their money into tax-free investments.
- When you marry, you may have to reorganise your investments to make them more tax-efficient.
- Investors over 65 on small incomes should bear in mind that the rules about reducing age allowance make it very important for them to take advantage of tax-free investments whenever possible, as the income they receive from these investments is not counted towards their total income for age allowance purposes.
- Don't forget that you can still ask for a refund if too much tax is deducted at source from investment income not subject to composite rate tax.
- Check up on all the ways in which claims for a refund of overpayment of tax concessions can be backdated – up to six years in some cases – so as to reduce your tax liabilities, especially if you have not taken up all the concessions available in the past. See p. 106 for an example of how you can do this with pension payments.
- It's easy to miss out on some of the more unusual reliefs – eg

interest reliefs on investment in small businesses. It's up to you to inform the tax inspector about this.
- If you are backdating tax reliefs, remember that you get the relief at the level in force at the time you are backdating it to, not the current levels.
- Check your tax bill.

Capital gains tax

You don't have to worry about capital gains tax unless you and your spouse together make profits of more than £6300 a year out of *selling* your investments (including some property). Capital gains tax is basically a tax on the increase in value of assets if you sell them, on the *difference* between what you paid for them and what you sell them for, with some allowance for inflation. It can also apply if you give away something valuable.

What assets qualify for capital gains tax?
Chargeable assets – those to which the tax applies – include stocks and shares, unit trust holdings, land, buildings, jewellery and antiques. However, there are a large number of exceptions. These include:

> Your own home;
> Private cars;
> Certain tax-free investments, such as National Savings;
> Lump sums received from pensions and some life insurance policies;
> Winnings from premium bonds and other lotteries including football pools and betting;
> Gifts to charities;
> Gifts between husband and wife;
> Chattels – personal possessions worth less than £3000 each, including antiques and jewellery.

If you are selling an item as part of your normal business activities, eg if you are an antique dealer, you pay income tax, not capital gains tax.

Who has to pay capital gains tax?
Anyone normally living in the United Kingdom, who makes more than £6300 profit by selling or otherwise disposing of chargeable assets both in this country and anywhere else in the world.

Anyone living abroad but doing business here who makes more

than £6300 profit out of the sale of business assets held in this country.

Capital gains tax does not have to be paid when property changes hands because of the owner's death.

Unfortunately, you can't escape paying the tax by *giving away* valuable possessions, because the Inland Revenue promptly charges you tax on the estimated difference between the market value when you gave it away, and the original price you paid. However, if the person receiving the gift agrees, payment of the capital gains tax due can be delayed until he or she disposes of the gift.

If an asset is destroyed or damaged, and you decide to keep the insurance money rather than replace the asset, you can be charged capital gains tax if you receive more compensation from the insurance company than the asset cost you in the first place.

How is capital gains tax calculated?

The tax is charged at a flat rate of 30 per cent on the net total of taxable gains above £6300 in any one year. Not the amount you sell assets for, but the amount of profit you make on the deal. There is a section in your annual tax return in which you have to notify the Inland Revenue of any chargeable gains and losses, if your total gain is over £6300. The Inland Revenue will then tell you how much you have to pay, and this is usually due by the end of December following the tax year in which you made the gain.

Don't forget that capital gains tax is on the *profit* you make out of increases in value. So you can set losses against gains, and also some of the costs involved in making the gain, for example, commission to stockbrokers, improvements, advertising the sale, but not routine maintenance and insurance. If you make a very substantial loss one year that puts you well below the £6300 limit, you can credit any excess loss against gains you make in the future. But you cannot backdate it to last year and get a rebate on tax already paid.

Example
You invest £10,000 in 10,000 shares in the South Sea Bubble Co in 1983. The share price takes off dramatically so you sell half your shares in 1984 for a net profit of £11,300. £6300 is tax free, but you have to pay CGT on the other £5000 at 30 per cent ie £1500. Alas, in 1985 the bubble bursts, and your remaining 5000 shares are worthless. You sell them to a man who collects dud share certificates as a hobby, so losing £5500 on your original investment, including costs. You have no capital gains in 1985, so you have in hand a loss of £5500 to set against any gain you make in 1986, or afterwards.

What about inflation?

Since 1982, some allowance for inflation has been built into the capital gains tax calculation. First, any asset held for at least one year before 6 April 1982 and sold after that date qualifies for an index-linked reduction in the amount of profit calculated for tax. So if, for example, the Retail Prices Index has gone up by 70 points from 310 at the end of March 1982 to 380 in the month when you sell the asset you can reduce the amount of taxable profit by the same proportion: $310 \div 380 = 81$ per cent – every £100-worth of gain is reduced to £81.

Any asset bought after the end of March 1982 qualifies for a similar reduction in the amount of taxable gain, related to the RPI. So if you bought shares in May 1984 and sell them in September 1985 you get 17 months' index-linking, using the May RPI as a base. If you bought the asset before April 1982 and sell it after April 1985, you can choose how to calculate the original price; the choice is between

the price you originally paid plus all the allowable expenses since then, or
the market value on March 31 1982 plus all allowable expenses since then.

You can choose which is most favourable to you, but you must notify the tax man.

Since April 1985 you can use the indexation allowances to turn a profit into a loss by index-linking, or to increase an existing loss.

The indexation rules began to operate from April 1982. Even if you bought the asset long before that, the indexation does not begin until that date.

Points to watch

- Use the rules about carrying forward losses to your best advantage.
- There are special rules for helping family businesses to cope with capital gains tax.
- Husband and wife can be assessed for capital gains and losses separately, but the total allowed tax free is still £6300 not £12,600.
- When you own two homes, you can choose which one is your 'main' home for tax purposes, if you notify the tax inspector within two years of purchasing the second home. So if you buy

a country cottage which you are more likely to sell again than your 'real' home, it may be worth declaring that house as your main residence, and so getting any profit on the sale tax free.

● If you know that you are likely to make considerable gains in one tax year, and few in the next, it could be worth trying to carry out the transactions either side of the end of the tax year, so they are spread over two years, rather than one. To put off the evil day as long as possible, delay carrying out a sale until after 6 April if you can, as then you would not have to pay any tax due until December the following year.

● Some investments do not qualify for capital gains tax. This gives them plus points if you are getting near the £6300 limit when deciding how to invest.

● Capital gains tax is charged at one flat rate, 30 per cent, so if you are paying income tax above the basic rate it may be better to go for capital gains rather than income when making your investments.

● Inland Revenue leaflets CGT 4, 8 and 12 give all the details about capital gains tax.

Capital transfer tax (inheritance tax)

The 1986 Budget proposed that the capital transfer tax should be substantially altered, so as to become, in effect, as the new name suggests, an inheritance tax. Even so, people who want to pass on some of their wealth to the family and friends will still find that there are some snags to giving their money away. Their heirs can be landed with a substantial tax bill if they aren't careful.

Inheritance tax will still be charged on gifts made during the last seven years of your life, and on the money and property you leave when you die.

What assets qualify for inheritance tax?
Any gifts of money, shares, property or other possessions may be liable for inheritance tax. Whether or not a gift is exempt normally depends on how much you gave away in your last seven years of life, and how large your estate is when you die. Some gifts are always tax free. These include:

● Gifts between husband and wife;
● Gifts to charities and to other worthy bodies;
● Gifts to political parties.

163

Who has to pay inheritance tax?

When anyone normally resident in the United Kingdom has given away more than £71,000 in the last seven years of his or her life, or when the estate amounts to more than £71,000, or when these two together come to over £71,000, their gifts and bequests may be subject to inheritance tax. Married couples are regarded as individuals for inheritance tax purposes, and husband and wife can each claim all the concessions and allowances.

If the person making a bequest also wants to pay any tax due on it, this is grossed up, with typical Inland Revenue ingenuity, so that the value of the bequest is deemed to include the tax payment too. This means that the amount of tax due is greater. So if you wanted to make a gift of £3000 and also to pay tax on it due at 15 per cent – £450 – you would have to pay out, not £3450, but £3529.41p.

Which? annual tax guide includes a very useful calculator to help you determine what your gift will be worth, taking this into account.

How is inheritance tax calculated?

When someone dies, the value of his or her estate will be 'cumulated' with any gifts made in the previous seven years. There are exemptions in addition to those mentioned above. These are: annual gifts of not more than £250 each to any number of individuals; wedding gifts – £5000 from a parent, £2500 from a grandparent or great grandparent, £1000 from anyone else.

In addition to these concessions, the first £3000 in any one year is also tax free.

Otherwise, taxable amounts you have given away in the last seven years are added on to the tax calculation of your estate. This is taxed at the following rates:

	On death %	Lifetime gifts %
£0-£71,000	Nil	Nil
£71,001-£95,000	30	15
£95,001-£129,000	35	17.5
£129,001-£164,000	40	20
£164,001-£206,000	45	22.5
£206,001-£257,000	50	25
£257,001-£317,000	55	27.5
Over £317,000	60	30

There is an additional concession according to when any taxable lifetime gift was made:

Years between gift and death	Percentage of full rate to be paid
Up to 3	100
3-4	80
4-5	60
5-6	40
6-7	20

There are special rules for gifts to trusts, and for some businesses and agricultural land. It will be up to the personal representatives of the person who has died to account for the gifts to the Revenue. The people who received any taxable lifetime gift have to pay the tax, but the Revenue can, if necessary, claim tax due from the estate.

These rules came into force from 18 March 1986, and the necessary forms can be obtained from the Capital Taxes Office:

Minford House, Rockley Road, London W14 0DF *(England and Wales)*
16 Picardy Place, Edinburgh EH1 3NB *(Scotland)*
Law Courts Building, Chichester Street, Belfast BT1 3NU *(Northern Ireland)*.

Inheritance tax: Points to watch

- If inheritance tax has to be paid on a gift, the amount paid is deducted from any capital gains tax due.
- If you are worth more than £50,000 taking into account all your investments and possessions, including your house, get professional advice.
- It is not difficult to plan in advance for inheritance tax, so don't make this an occasion for deathbed repentance.
- Because the rules are changing some gifts made before March 1986 may now be subject to inheritance tax. There will be transitional provisions so that people do not have to pay more than they would have done under the old system.

Corporation tax

Any limited company making a profit has to pay corporation tax on its net profits. The rate goes up according to how large the profits are. Some financial institutions such as insurance companies are exempt from tax on profits or pay tax in a different way which gives them an advantage over companies which have to pay full rates of tax.

Companies have to pay *advanced corporation tax* (ACT) on the dividends they distribute to shareholders. They have to pay the Inland Revenue three-sevenths of the gross amount paid out in dividends within three months of its being distributed to shareholders. This is deducted from the gross amount of corporation tax due at the end of the year.

The shareholder receives the dividend less the three-sevenths tax and is credited with having paid tax at the basic rate on the dividends received. This is called the *imputation* system. So if you are entitled to a dividend of £100, you receive £71 and are also given a tax credit of 29/71sts of that amount = £29 = basic rate tax.

Franked income

When a unit or investment trust receives dividends from companies in the United Kingdom in which it holds shares, these dividends would normally be paid net of tax, with the advanced corporation tax already deducted. If corporation tax were to be charged on this money again before being passed on to share- or unit-holders in the trust, it would mean that the same income had been taxed twice. So the trust is allowed to calculate its tax liability taking the tax paid on this *franked income* into account.

Income that has not already paid tax is known as *unfranked income* and tax on this has to be accounted for before it is distributed to shareholders.

As far as share- or unit-holders are concerned, there is no practical difference. They receive their dividends with the equivalent of basic rate tax deducted, and the Inland Revenue credit them with this tax in the normal way.

Stamp duty

Stamp duty is the collective name given to a range of taxes on legal documents, on buying a house costing over £30,000 for example, or the transfer of shares. The *transfer stamp duty* on the transfer of shares from one owner to another is charged at the flat rate of 1 per cent on all purchases (sellers do not have to pay it), reducing to 0.5 per cent from 27 October 1986. Gilt-edged securities and some other loan stocks are exempt from the tax. Unit and investment trusts have to pay it on some purchases, but the cost is accounted for in the spread between bid and offer price.

Value added tax (VAT)

This affects the investor in two main ways. First, you have to pay VAT on services rendered to you by a stockbroker or other dealer on which he charges commission. So VAT is added to the bill the stockbroker sends you. VAT is also payable on management charges made by unit trust companies and other fund managers, but this is accounted for in the annual charges they take out of the funds; you don't get a personal bill for it.

Second, you may have to pay VAT when you are investing in things, gold coins or jewellery for example. This is charged on the full price when the object bought is new. Because of the difficulties in calculating VAT on something that is not new when you buy or sell it, there are special rules for dealing in second-hand goods, which would include antiques, pictures etc. Basically, VAT is charged on the dealer's mark-up, not on the full price – on the difference between what the dealer paid for it and what it is sold for.

Covenants

A covenant is a legally binding agreement to make regular payments to another person out of your income. Because you are legally making over the money to someone else, it no longer counts as part of your income and you no longer have to pay tax on the covenanted amounts.

Either you or the person you have covenanted the money to can reclaim the tax paid at the basic rate from the Inland Revenue. So if you covenant £1 to Oxfam, the charity can get £1.40 – £1 plus basic rate tax at 29 per cent grossed up – because it can recover 40p from the Inland Revenue, the cost to you in tax to have £1 to dispose of. You must, yourself, be paying tax.

If you covenant £100 to a student daughter, this costs you £71 because your tax bill is reduced by tax on £100 at basic rate – £29.

The tax can be reclaimed only at the basic rate, no matter what rate of tax you pay, except that if you pay higher rates of tax you can deduct any money covenanted to *charities* – not to individuals – from your income assessment and so reduce your tax bill at the higher rates.

It is only worth making a covenant to an individual if the person receiving the covenanted money (and their spouse if any) does not pay income tax. Money received from covenants counts as investment income, and is subject to income tax in the normal way. Charities don't pay income tax.

Most people realise that it's worth doing this for a student son or daughter. The National Union of Students has a helpful leaflet telling you how, price 50p plus large stamped-addressed envelope available from Education and Welfare Department, 461 Holloway Road, London N7 6LJ.

You can't covenant to your own children until they are 18 or over, but it may be worthwhile to make covenanted gifts to other people's children – grandchildren or godchildren, for example – as long as they don't have enough income of their own to pay tax. The tax man will smell a rat if you make a reciprocal agreement with a friend to covenant to each other's children, but you could use a covenant to build up a nice little nest egg, through an insurance policy perhaps, for a grandchild.

Chapter 11

Interest

'he rails
On me, my bargain and my well-won thrift,
Which he calls interest'.

(Merchant of Venice)

Everyone grudges paying interest, so perhaps that is why there is some reluctance among small investors to look around for the best bargains in interest rates. It may explain why people persist in keeping their money in low-paying investments when they could get a much better deal elsewhere.

Although the word *interest* is often used to mean any kind of return or income that you get from an investment, it should, strictly speaking, be kept for the extra regular payments you receive in return for making a loan to someone, the cost of the loan to the borrower. Shares do not pay interest; they pay you an annual *dividend*, a share of the profits, if any, the company has made. Some investments pay no interest at all; the return they provide is an increase in the value of the sum of money you have invested – capital growth. For example, if you buy a house for £15,000 and sell it for £30,000 your capital investment has grown by £15,000. Many investments provide both income and capital growth. If you buy shares, for instance, you hope to receive a dividend each year, and also to be able to sell the shares at a profit in due course.

If you receive a high income from an investment it's unlikely that the capital you have invested in it will be increasing very much in value. If you receive very little interest, you ought to get a worthwhile amount of capital growth; if you don't, put your money somewhere more profitable.

Interest rates

The rates of interest paid on an investment depend on the kind of investment it is, and the general level of interest rates. The City of

London is a highly sophisticated money market, which revolves around the Bank of England. The Bank, as 'lender of last resort' will always lend or borrow money from the market – at a price. This means that the government can influence interest rates generally by the rate it is charging or paying financial institutions. You will see press comment like, 'Hopes for a cut in interest rates were disappointed in the absence of any encouragement from the Bank of England.'

The Bank and the government do not have it all their own way, however. What happens on the New York Exchange, or in Switzerland, or any major trading nation, has its effect on the London market, which cannot afford to ignore the rest of the world. If our rates are too high 'hot money' comes in from abroad, and may leave just as quickly. If the rates are too low, investors will prefer to take their money elsewhere. Time differences mean that the New York Exchange finishes some five hours later than London, before Tokyo has hardly begun, so the financial scene can change overnight.

Bearing in mind all these activities, the main London clearing banks will set their own base rates, which don't normally differ very much one from another. The base rate influences most other lending and borrowing rates on the market, so a cut in the base rate is usually followed by a cut in building society, local authority and National Savings rates. Some are quicker to change than others, and some may have to give notice to investors before making any change. You can see that it is as well to keep an eye on what is going on in the markets if you want to get the best interest for your money.

How is interest calculated?

Interest rates are almost always given as the percentage paid annually on the amount you have invested. So a nominal rate of 11 per cent pays £11 each year for every £100 invested. Interest rates may be *fixed*, ie they remain the same for the whole time that you keep the investment regardless of what happens on the money markets, or *variable*: they go up and down according to the state of the market. It's not always easy to tell which is which from some of the advertisements put out by the financial institutions. The word *guaranteed* can be deceptive. It could mean that the rate is guaranteed to remain the same throughout the term of the investment. More often it means that the rate will be a fixed amount – say 2 per cent – higher than other rates. So if base rate falls by half of 1 per cent to 10 per cent, the guaranteed interest rate will fall correspondingly from 12½ to 12 per cent. If it rises, the guaranteed rate rises too, whereas a fixed rate would remain the same.

An important factor is the period over which the amount of interest due is calculated. Some investments pay interest only on complete calendar months, so you get no interest for the months in which you pay in or draw out your money. Others calculate the interest for every day in which your money remains invested. These complications would not apply to fixed-term investments as the time for which you promise to lend the money is clear from the start. Some investments, in particular National Savings, have a qualifying period before you begin to earn any interest.

Loss of interest

Many investments specify a period of notice that must be given before you can withdraw your money. There may be interest penalties if you take your money out before the agreed term is up, or without the required period of notice. Some companies will not allow you to do this at all (unless you die, in which case it's not much help to you); but there is so much competition that most schemes have some escape clause if you *must* have the money. Penalties may include:

● Loss of extra interest above the ordinary rate. This may come as a shock if you have been taking out the interest instead of re-investing it. Because you have been getting interest at a higher rate on the understanding that you would leave your money in for a fixed term, you may find that the company calculates what you would have earned at the ordinary rate, and deducts the difference when it pays you back your capital.

Say you were getting 11.5 per cent on £5000 on the basis that you'd keep the money in for five years. Once a year you'd taken out your £575 interest, but after three years you need the £5000 unexpectedly. So the company would say 'Ah, but then you are entitled to 8.75 per cent only on that money for those three years, ie £437.50 a year. We've paid you £1725 altogether, and you should have had £1312.50, so we're deducting the extra £412.50 from your original investment of £5000 and paying you £4587.50 back.'

They would make the same kind of calculation if you had re-invested the interest instead of withdrawing it, with the result that the total amount of capital and interest paid to you would be reduced.

● No interest paid from date of notice of withdrawal. This can be quite a big loss. For example, suppose you have to give three months' notice of withdrawal. You get no interest on the money during that three months, so if you had £3000 invested at 10.75 per cent for one year, you get less interest than you would have received from keeping the money in an ordinary account at 8.75 per cent.

● Loss of 28 or more days' interest if full notice not given.

● No interest at all if you withdraw early – during the first year of SAYE schemes, for example.

When is interest paid?

The most common way of paying interest is for the interest due to be calculated twice a year, and at the end of each half-year either added to the sum you have invested, or paid direct to you. This may be done monthly for some larger investments, or only once a year in some cases. When the returns on different investments are compared, it is usually assumed that the interest or dividend is added to the sum invested (or *accumulated*) and in the next interest period the interest due is calculated on the new amount. This is called the compounded annual rate (CAR). Since the invention of the calculator the process of working out compound interest is no longer the burden it used to be.

It does make a difference whether the interest is paid yearly or half-yearly. Half-yearly is better because at the end of the second half you get a half-year's interest on the interest credited at the end of the first six months, as well as on the original sum.

Example
You invest £1000 in a building society at 8.5 per cent a year. If the interest is paid yearly you get £85 at the end of one year. If it is paid half-yearly you get £42.50 at the end of the first six months, so the sum invested becomes £1042.50 for the second six months, and you get £44.30 interest for the second half – a total of £86.50. This is almost one-fifth of 1 per cent more.

How is interest taxed?

Interest is now usually taxed at the *composite* rate, as explained on p. 158. If *basic* rate tax has been deducted before you receive the money, you should receive a tax credit or tax deduction certificate from the institution paying the interest. *Tax credits* apply when the company pays advance corporation tax, and tax at the basic rate is *imputed* to you; *tax deduction certificates* apply when the company has simply deducted the amount due under basic rate tax. It makes no difference to the amount you receive or the amount of basic rate tax you are considered to have paid.

Basic rate taxpayers have no more to worry about as far as tax is concerned. However, you may have more to pay if, when the income is grossed up as explained on p. 158, your income is subject to higher rates of tax or age allowance.

What matters to the individual is what an investment pays *after* allowing for your personal tax position. A non-taxpayer ought to look at interest rates very differently from someone paying high rates of tax. For example, an investment of £1000 that pays 12½ per cent without deduction of tax is worth £125 to the non-taxpayer, but only £50 to someone paying at the top rate of 60 per cent.

When the basic rate is 29 per cent then the grossed up rate can be calculated by multiplying the net interest rate by 1.40. So 8.75 per cent net of tax = 12.25 per cent to the basic rate taxpayer. If you pay at a higher rate, you can calculate your rate of return by multiplying the grossed-up rate by your own rate of return after tax. For example, someone paying 40 per cent tax gets six-tenths of any interest received – 0.6. If you multiply 12.5 by 0.6, the result is 7.5; so 12.5 per cent gross is worth 7.5 per cent to the 40 per cent taxpayer.

Tax rate	Rate of return net of tax	Value of 12½% interest rate
45%	0.55	6.875%
50%	0.50	6.25%
55%	0.45	5.625%
60%	0.40	5.00%

Points to watch

● Read the small print about how the interest is calculated.
● Check the penalties for early withdrawal.
● Don't be tempted by high interest rates into taking on commit-

ments that you may not be able to keep up. You may find that you would have been better off settling for a lower rate and fewer penalties.

- When interest rates look likely to fall, fixed-interest rates can be a bargain. Some institutions take a month or two to alter their rates, so you may be able to catch them before the rate has changed.
- Even though you have to pay tax on interest, it's still worth shopping around for the best bargain. For example, 11.5 per cent from the National Savings Investment account is still better for the basic rate taxpayer than 7 per cent tax-paid from the building society.
- Remember that interest counts as investment income, and as such is added to your spouse's income for tax purposes. So if one partner is in a high tax bracket, the other should choose tax-free investments for savings if possible.

Chapter 12
Financial Advice

'And may ye better reck the rede
    Than ever did th'adviser'.
                            Robert Burns, 'Epistle to a Young Friend'

The best advice you can get is to buy yourself a calculator, unless you already have one, and learn how to use it. It takes all the hardship out of the many calculations you need to do in order to invest your money sensibly. You don't have to be a mathematical genius, and you don't have to buy one of those machines that need a mathematical genius to understand the keyboard. All you want is a simple little pocket calculator that can add, subtract, divide, multiply, do percentages, and has a memory. It should not cost more than a few pounds and you'll be surprised at the fun you can have with it.

In fact, you are potentially your own best financial adviser. Nobody else knows half as much as you about your real needs and wishes, and no one else has such a direct personal interest in advising you successfully. After all, if these advisers are so successful, why are they still selling advice for a living, rather than administering their own millions?

That's not to say that you can't learn a lot from the many sources of financial advice available, or that you never need professional help. But unless you understand what the advice means to you personally, you are not going to get the best out of it.

Investment advisers

Surveys of the advice offered by investment advisers have produced rather negative results and very little evidence that it is worth paying their fees. One problem is that the field is so wide it may be unreasonable to expect one person to cover all the possibilities. An adviser also needs to know a good deal about your financial affairs before recommending any course of action, as well as fairly obvious points like your age, income and family responsibilities. The adviser, to do the job properly, would need to know details of all your existing insurance, pension and other investments, your outgoings and the pattern of your expenditure, what the future is likely to hold, and your temperament – are you prepared to take risks, for example? That's why the better you and the adviser know one another, the better the advice is likely to be.

You can go to an adviser for general or specific advice and then carry out the transactions yourself. Or you can ask for advice, make your decision, and then ask him to buy or sell the investment for you, in which case he will probably charge a fee. Another choice is to hand over your portfolio to the adviser for him to manage on your behalf for a fee. You can either give him the discretion to buy or sell investments as he thinks fit or ask to be consulted before any decisions are taken.

If you are going to hand over your portfolio to others to manage, it is common sense to make sure that they belong to an established firm with sound financial backing. Advisers who are members of well-regulated professions such as the law and accountancy will have a duty to maintain professional standards, and there will probably be some kind of compensation fund to protect you against business failure. The same protection may not be available in other cases.

Anyone buying or selling securities to the public has to have a Department of Trade and Industry licence. This also applies to anyone who offers advice on buying and selling investments. All *licensed dealers* have to keep clients' money and investments in an account separate from the firm's own money. This means that if the firm runs into trouble, and goes bankrupt, the client does not risk losing all the money put into the firm's keeping. Advisers must have formal contracts with their clients, especially if they are acting as investment managers, and buying and selling on their behalf. They must disclose any personal interest in any investment they recommend (such as payment of commission), and if there is a possible conflict of interest, the client's consent must be obtained in writing. The adviser must keep proper records and notify the client of transactions undertaken for him or her.

The National Association of Securities Dealers and Investment Managers (NASDIM) require their members to take out insurance to compensate clients for loss arising from fraud or negligence by them or their employees. Because of the strict conditions of membership of NASDIM, their members are allowed to practise without individual DTI licences.

Compensation funds protect you against business failures and fraud, but it is very unlikely that you could get compensation just because you lost money by taking advice. Advisers must have been professionally negligent for you to have any claim against them. To succeed in a claim you would probably have to show that a reasonable person would not have given the advice – quite difficult to prove.

Don't forget that many advisers are paid commission by the insurance firm or other investment company if they sell you an investment. If they do not charge fees to clients the commission is their only source of income, and it is as well to be aware that the advice they give may not be completely impartial.

Banks. Your bank manager can give you advice, often free, about your immediate financial affairs, and can call on the vast range of specialist services offered by the big banks, at a price. Banks will also be prepared to act as trustees, buy stocks and shares for you etc. They are sometimes criticised for charging a lot to look after small investors' portfolios, and you would not expect them to be anything other than conservative in their choices.

Solicitors. Although solicitors are trained in the law rather than finance, they are often a source of advice on sorting out financial affairs, and may be prepared to look after your investments and buy and sell for you. They should be able to put you in touch with the appropriate experts and will charge the usual consultation fees.

Accountants are trained to keep track of money and in the principles of investment and tax law generally, though not specifically on investment advice for the individual. They may be willing to look after your portfolio, and buy and sell for you, and may be more aware of the different opportunities than bank managers or solicitors.

Insurance brokers ought to be able to give full advice about any aspect of insurance and pensions, and may give general advice about other investments. Make sure they are registered with the Brokers' Registration Council.

Investment consultants. Although there are now more statutory controls over investment consultants, it is not difficult to set up as one, and the quality of advice given varies very widely. You need to be sure that you are getting impartial general advice about a spread of investments, as many consultants are specialists in one area, often insurance, and may give inadequate advice about other kinds of investment.

Financial companies. Many of the City firms who run unit trusts and insurance companies offer an advice and management service to people with enough money to invest to make it worth their while. In practice this means about £25,000. For analysing your portfolio, making recommendations about your investments and carrying them out, and giving advice on related financial matters, a group would probably charge about 1 per cent of the total sum invested in a year.

Finance and the media

Financial affairs probably get more and better coverage than any other aspect of the news. Every daily newspaper has its financial column, and gives some attention to the latest stock market prices. Changes in the interest rate always hit the headlines. There is a wealth of information and comment freely, or almost freely, available, not just in the editorial columns, but also in the advertisements that fill the financial pages. It all helps you to keep up to date with what's going on.

Newspapers

You can't claim to be a serious investor unless you read the *Financial Times* regularly. If you jib at the idea of making it your daily newspaper (though its coverage of the arts and media is very good) you ought at least to read the Saturday issue, which has a summary of all the week's main financial news, and several feature pages on *Finance and the family*.

In addition to the daily newspaper, the FT has an unrivalled financial information service, which helps to produce the FT Actuaries Indices – an essential part of any investor's tool kit. They consist of a series of summaries of movements in stocks and shares compiled jointly by the FT, the Institute of Actuaries and the Faculty of Actuaries. The indices are compiled for different groups of shares, or stocks, for representative groups, and for All-Shares, which covers altogether 739 shares. They are used as a measure of stock market performance, and to pinpoint different areas of growth. A commentator might say, 'The FT Industrial Share Index moved up 2.4 points today', which means that the index price of a group of industrial shares representing the whole gamut of the industrial share market has gone up from, say, 373.36 to 375.76. Within that group the Index for Food Retailing may have gone down, while the Chemicals Index may have gone up more than 2.4. The FT-SE 100 Share Index represents the most recent attempt to draw up an index that gives a reliable measure of the state of the market generally.

The indices also provide a useful standard of comparison. You can, for example, look to see if the unit trust company you patronise has done worse or better than the relevant FT Share Index.

You can phone 01-246 8026 for a recorded message from the FT giving you the latest share prices and business news, updated hourly. The Financial Times Business Publishing Company also publishes a range of useful handbooks and yearbooks.

Most of the other quality papers print daily lists of share prices and reports on financial dealings, and have a weekly Saturday feature on family money and investment. These will normally give up-to-date information about interest rates and conditions for most of the investments that appeal to the small investor. The *Daily Telegraph* has a particularly detailed table of investment returns. The *Guardian* will give you a slightly different slant on the financial news from the other quality papers. The *Sunday Times* and the *Observer* both have pull-out supplements on business news full of helpful and informative comment and information.

Magazines

There are almost as many magazines with financial commentaries as there are newspapers. Most people are aware of the established and widely available weeklies like the *Economist* and *Investors Chronicle* but here is a quick guide to a few of the more specialised periodicals likely to be of interest to the small investor:

Money Management is a monthly sold mainly on subscription (£42.50 a year first class post, £36 second class). It is the bible for investment trade professionals and a source of much of the factual information and surveys used by other financial journalists. It offers a weekly rate update service which keeps you informed of all the changes in the various rates during the week. This costs £180 a year. Subscriptions from Money Management Magazine, Greystoke Place, London EC4B 40J; tel: 01-405 6969.

Money Observer is an offshoot of the *Observer*'s business section. It's a full-scale monthly magazine, available on subscription only £17.50 a year). It contains regular features on unit and investment trusts, building societies, and stocks and shares, aimed at both professional and amateur investors. It's very good at setting out the bones of a subject and giving novices about all they need to know to begin thinking about it; available from Subscription Services Department, The Money Observer, 120-126 Lavender Avenue, Mitcham, Surrey CR4 3HP.

Which? magazine no longer publishes their *Money Which?* supplement. Instead, regular articles on money matters, savings and investment appear regularly in the main magazine throughout the year. It's an excellent source of unbiased, clear-headed, easily understood, if sometimes pedestrian, advice. *Which?*, 1 Caxton Hill, Hertford SG13 7LZ; tel: Hertford 57773.

Planned Savings is a monthly (subscription £38 a year first class, £33 second class) that does for the small investor what *Money Management* does for the professionals. Its surveys and reviews of performance are particularly useful. Other magazines published by the group include *Pensions Magazine* (£25 a year first class and £22 second class) and *Savings Market* (£43 a year first class, £40 second class). These magazines are published by United Trade Press at 33-35 Bowling Green Lane, London EC1R 0DA; tel: 01-837 1212.

Television and radio
In addition to news coverage – the 6 o'clock news on BBC Radio 4, for instance, always includes a stock market report – there is the daily *Financial World Tonight* at 11.15 pm and magazine programmes dealing with financial and investment topics, such as *Money Matters* and *Money Box* on Radio 4 and the *Money Programme* on BBC TV.

The teletext services on BBC and ITV contain pages with the latest information on share prices and other news, and Prestel offers all kinds of financial information. Many libraries now offer a Prestel service if you don't have access to it at home or at work.

Libraries

Most reference libraries will have some kind of financial and legal section, and the better ones are a good source of financial information, including company reports and all the financial press. They may subscribe to the Extel card system which gives brief details of the latest information on, for example, dividends, P/E ratios and annual reports for most public companies.

If you haven't a good business reference library near home, perhaps at a local business college or university, it may be worth making a trip to the City Business Library at 55 Basinghall Street, London EC2V 5DX near Moorgate tube station, tel: 01-638 8215. The library is open Monday-Friday from 9.30 am to 5 pm, and has the comprehensive stock of publications and other information sources you would expect from its title.

Share shops

Share shops and Money Centres are bringing the stock market and other financial dealings to the High Street. You can, for example, walk into a share shop and buy and sell shares over the counter. Deals can be recorded by computer immediately through the Stock Exchange Automated Quotation network (SEAQ). Investment advice may also be available, at a price. Before using a share shop, it is advisable to find out about its backing, and whether, for example, it has formal links with the Stock Exchange, which would offer some protection against fraud.

Investor protection

The Financial Services Bill, published in 1985, is making its laborious way through the Houses of Parliament, subject to many amendments as it goes. It is expected to become law at the end of 1986. It provides for a Securities and Investment Board (SIB) to supervise a group of new Self Regulatory Organisations (SROs) for different areas of investment. These will lay down proper standards of conduct for people operating in their area and will also provide protection against fraud and insolvency for the individual investor. They will either have their own compensation fund, or will contribute to a central fund run by the SIB. The Stock Exchange will continue to be responsible for dealing in securities, and NASDIM (see p. 176) will also continue. New SROs will look after international securities, futures, investment managers, and insurance-linked investments.

Chapter 13

Financial Jargon

'When I use a word,' Humpty Dumpty said in a rather scornful tone, 'it means just what I choose it to mean – neither more nor less.'
Lewis Carroll, *Through the Looking Glass*

You could probably compile a dictionary as long as the *Shorter Oxford* explaining what the financial experts choose their words to mean, but this brief list discusses a few of the commonly used words, not explained elsewhere in the text, that sometimes confuse the beginner.

Assets

Anything you have that is worth something to you is an asset, the opposite being a *liability*, which is anything you have that is going to cost you money. Your assets might consist of a house, a car, furniture, a stereo, a few National Savings Certificates, some savings in a building society, some cash in your pocket and some money in a bank account. Liabilities might be a mortgage, a hire purchase loan on the car, and money owing on a credit card or the telephone bill.

A company's assets are usually classified as *fixed assets* – any buildings, other property, machinery, cars and lorries, plus, possibly, the 'goodwill' built up over the years by the firm; and *current assets* – stocks of materials, money owing to it for goods or services already supplied, money at the bank or in the petty cash. Its liabilities could be loans raised from the public, an overdraft at the bank, bills not yet paid, and unpaid taxes due to the Inland Revenue.

Among the *current liabilities*, first and foremost is the bank overdraft, because that can be called in at any time. Tax bills and trade creditors come next; loans from the public are not normally due for repayment in the short term.

Balance sheet

If you list the value of all your assets and all your liabilities, and deduct the total liabilities from the total of assets, this is your personal balance sheet and what's left is your net capital.

A company's balance sheet sets out the same details, so as to give a true picture of the company's general financial state at the end of the working year. When you deduct the liabilities from the assets, what's left belongs to the shareholders of the company.

There are all kinds of tests applied by the analysts to check up on the health of a company as demonstrated by the balance sheet. One that anyone can understand is the ratio of current liabilities to current assets, in other words, are there enough resources to pay off short-term debts? A more severe version of the same test is the *acid test* ratio which measures the current liabilities against the assets that could be turned into cash immediately if necessary. This would not include stocks, for example, because you might not be able to sell them at a good price in a hurry.

The acid test is a particularly important one for small businesses. Many collapse, not because they would not be profitable in the long run, but because they haven't enough cash to pay next week's bills.

Bulls and bears

These are creatures that inhabit the stock markets. You can remember which is which by the simple clue that bulls toss prices up while bears bear down on them – push them down. Bulls buy shares when they believe that the price is about to rise, so they will be able to sell at a higher price than they paid. Bears think that prices are going down, so they sell shares hoping to be able to buy them back at a lower price later on.

So a 'bull' market is a market where prices are rising. If the market looks 'bearish' prices may be about to fall.

Capital

'Accumulated wealth applied reproductively' says the dictionary; in other words, savings that are being used in such a way that they increase in value.

For investors, the most important distinction is between capital and income. Capital is the lump sum or regular savings that you pay into an investment, and income is the interest or dividends you receive as a reward for giving up your money. All sorts of influences combine to eat away at your capital. You may have chosen a bad investment so that when the time comes to sell you get less than you paid for it. You may find that although you get the same amount back in cash terms, in real terms rising prices mean that it is not worth as much as when you bought the investment. On the other hand, if you make a good choice, the capital will be worth more when you take it out than when you invested it.

From the company point of view, *capital* has more specialised meanings. When a company, however small, is formed, it must have an *authorised share capital*, or *nominal* capital, which very approximately represents the value put into the company by the founders. Some shares belong to the original owners, others may be sold to new shareholders, but not all the shares in the authorised capital have to be issued at once. Those that are issued form the *paid up capital*. Once the authorised amount of shares has been issued, it needs a change in the company's rules, approved by the shareholders, to increase the authorised capital and issue more shares. In time, if the company prospers, the value of the assets it owns is far higher than the authorised capital; similarly, the value of the shares may be far higher than the nominal price.

Then there is *working capital*, which is the money turning over to keep the business going – it represents the same figure, roughly speaking, as current assets minus current liabilities.

Contango

This is a technical term which means paying a bit extra to avoid having to pay now. It is specifically applied to dealing in stocks and shares, which have to be settled within the account period (see p. 59). On Contango day, the last day of the account, you can arrange a Contango on a deal you have made so that settlement can be delayed into the next account period.

Contangos are also relevant in some commodity purchases where you pay more for delivery on a future date, because the delay will cost the seller money if he has to store the goods for you, and if the market changes. The opposite of Contango is *backwardation* – a premium the *seller* has to pay for the privilege of not delivering the stock or goods until a later settlement day.

Discount

As well as the common meaning of *discount* – a reduction in the normal price – this word expresses the way in which the market takes into account various future events when calculating the price of a stock or share, eg the fact that the dividend is about to be paid.

When new share issues are made, the price is said to be at a *discount* if the offer price is less than the nominal or face value, and at a *premium* if the price is higher than the face value.

Gearing

Gearing is the financial term for borrowing to increase profits – the more borrowing the higher the gearing. You could say that banks are very highly geared because they lend out far more money in the form of overdrafts than they hold in their coffers, and customer accounts. The money they make from interest on these overdrafts – on lending money they haven't got – increases their profits very considerably.

Companies borrow perhaps to finance a new factory that will increase their production and sales, and so make more profits. The crunch comes if the expected profits do not materialise and the firm still has to pay interest on the extra loans. So the amount of gearing a company has is of great interest to the financial commentators, and to anyone considering investing or lending money to a firm. Too little, and it may be moving too slowly; too much, and it may outrun its strength.

Hedging

You hedge your bets by backing more than one horse, but hedging in the stock markets is a slightly more sophisticated form of insurance whereby you balance out your dealings by arranging, for example, a matching contract to buy with one to sell. A typical hedging transaction is to buy some shares which you hope will go up in price, and at the same time buy an option to sell them at a fixed price later on. If the price does not rise you have your option to sell to fall back on. Many complicated investment strategies can be built up on this simple foundation.

Index-linking

Index-linking is a development that arose from the high inflation rates of the last 20 years. It is an attempt to anticipate and compensate for the risk that inflation will destroy the value of capital. This risk makes people unwilling to lend money for long periods except at very high interest rates, which in themselves cause more inflation.

When savings are index-linked, the value of the capital is linked to an index of prices, usually the Retail Prices Index which covers all the main costs that affect a family budget. So when you get your money back, the capital will be increased along with inflation so that it is still worth the same in real terms as it was when you lent it.

When inflation rates fall, and it looks as if prices are going to be more stable in the future, index-linked investments are not as popular as those offering a reasonable rate of return from interest or dividends.

Indices
(singular Index)

An index is a convenient way of measuring changes over a wide range of prices, for example, the FT Indices discussed on p. 178. It saves individual investors or dealers the trouble of working out many different and complicated changes in price for themselves, and gives an independent basis for making comparisons.

When an index is first established, the base line is normally 100 and the various prices that index covers are each weighted according to their importance. For example, an index of building costs might give the highest weighting to labour costs. Then each time the index is revalued, the percentage increases and decreases in the various component prices are fed in so as to produce an overall percentage increase or decrease. The Retail Prices Index, for instance, was launched in January 1974 at 100. In December 1985 it stood at 378.9, a rise of 18.1 points over the last 12 months.

Liquidity

To be liquid in financial terms means to hold plenty of cash and short-term investments instead of long-term investments that cannot easily be cashed in. So the *liquidity ratio* is the ratio of cash in hand and at the bank to liabilities. If it is too low, the company may be in danger of going bankrupt because it can't pay the bills. If it is too high, the company may be passing up the chance of using that cash in a productive way.

When prices are very unsettled, a unit or investment trust may maintain a high liquidity ratio because it won't want to risk losing money by paying too high a price for stocks and shares. However, the cash will not be held in a current account: it will be on short-term deposit earning interest.

Portfolio

A portfolio is a bag used for carrying papers about, and so it came to be used as shorthand for the documents themselves. In investment terms, it means the spread of investments held by an individual or an institution, such as a pension fund or insurance company.

Much investment advice concentrates on giving guidelines as to the ideal portfolio for the cautious investor, the risk-taking investor etc, showing you how to arrange the distribution of your investments to meet your needs.

Yield

The yield is the total return you get from an investment taking into account any increase in the value of the capital plus any interest or dividends you receive while you hold it. It is usually expressed as an annual percentage of the going price and it's often assumed that any interest or dividend received will be re-invested.

The yield may be expressed in different ways; *gross yield* is usually the total received in interest or dividends without deduction of tax; *gross redemption yield* is the same sum plus any increase in the value of the capital because you get back more than you paid for it, *net yield* is the amount received in dividends or interest after tax has been deducted at the basic rate.

So a £1 share selling at 175 that pays a net dividend of 10.17p has a gross yield of 8.4 per cent.

A short life stock, eg LCC 5½ per cent 82.84 selling at 93, has a gross yield of 5.91, a gross redemption yield of 9.89 per cent.

Part Three
How to make your choice

It's no good looking for definitive answers in this section. You can't tell your fortune from a book, but you should find some precepts to help you influence what that fortune will be.

Chapter 14

Be Your Own Adviser

'As soon as questions of will or decision or reason or choice of action arise, human science is at a loss.'

Noam Chomsky

Although an investment adviser seldom admits to being at a loss, the ups and downs of the economy make it perilous even to attempt to give advice in a book. By the time the book is published, there could have been a change in the economic scene like the one that took place in 1982 when we switched from a high interest economy, where the person with money to lend could pick and choose from a variety of high returns, to one where interest rates and inflation fell dramatically and investors couldn't wait to cash in their index-linked Granny Bonds. Yet who could say for certain how long interest rates would remain low?

The Stock Exchange itself is a telling example of the basic irrationality of investment choices; its rises and falls are openly ascribed to 'market sentiment', and often have very little real relationship to the profitability of the companies whose shares are being bought and sold. So instead of *telling* you what to do, this part of the book asks you what you want to do, and at the same time sets out to explain what the consequences of that particular choice might be. This is done by asking you a series of questions based on the information about the various different kinds of investment given in Part One. Your answers to these questions should help you make up your mind how to invest your money. Some examples of different kinds of investment, all of which are fully discussed in Part One, are given for each category of answer.

In the end, it has to be your decision.

1. How much do you have to invest?

Although this might seem to be a question of fundamental importance, it does not, in fact, affect your choice as much as you would expect, even though some investments have to be ruled out if you cannot stump up the minimum sum required (see Question 4). If you haven't much to start with, you should be able to put by a little every week or month until you have enough to launch out more boldly. Those proverbs about many a mickle making a muckle do, like most old adages, have some truth in them.

Few of us are in the happy position of being able to live on our investment income; it's much more a matter of how we want our savings to enhance our standard of living or our peace of mind. That's why the answers to the other questions are more significant than the simple 'How much have you got?'. However, it is necessary to work out how much you have to invest with, so the two basic questions are:

(a) How big a lump sum do you have to invest?

(b) How much would you save regularly?

2. How long do you want to invest it for?

Having worked out how much you have, you then need to decide how long it will be before you need the money back. It's difficult to get out of long-term investments early without losing money, but short-term investments may pay less well. So make up your mind about how much you can tie up for a long time and how much you ought to keep easily accessible.

If you need cash quickly, for some emergency, you may lose money if you can't wait to sell until the market is in your favour.

a) Are you saving for some special purpose – a holiday, a car, a house? Is there a time limit by which you must have the cash?

b) Are you saving for a rainy day? If so what's the weather forecast? Does your income fluctuate a good deal, so that it would be difficult to keep up regular payments? Is anything likely to happen that might stop you keeping regular payments, eg losing your job? Can you foresee any crisis when you would need the money in a hurry?

c) Are you saving for retirement? What kind of pension arrangements do you have? Do you need to add to them?

Examples
Short term

Suitable for both lump sums and regular savings	National Savings Investment account. Bank deposits. Building Society ordinary shares.

Medium term	
Lump sums	Local authority loans. Building society bond schemes. Single premium life insurance policies.
Regular savings	National Savings Yearly Plan. Building society and bank savings schemes.
Both lump sum and regular savings	National Savings Certificates.
Long term	
Lump sum	Property.
Regular savings	Endowment insurance policies.
Both lump sum and regular savings	Unit and investment trusts. Personal pension plans.

3. How safe must your money be?

The choice is between:

- Having a guarantee that you will get all your money back;
- Having a guarantee that you will get the real value of your money back allowing for inflation;
- Accepting some degree of risk that you could lose money.

You pay for safety just as you pay for anything else, so an index-linked investment, for example, that guarantees you will get back the real purchasing power of the money you paid in, generally pays little or no interest.

It can't be said too often that all investments linked in any way to the prices of stocks and shares or other market prices carry some risk, no matter how well the investment has done in the past. So be wary of the glowing prospects projected by many insurance and unit trust companies on the basis of past performance. The first law of investment is that prices can go down as well as up.

There's no harm in taking risks as long as you are aware of what you are doing. If you are hoping to make big gains, you are unlikely to do this with safe investments.

a) How much money can you *afford* to lose?

b) How much money do you *mind* losing?

c) Is inflation-proofing in the long term more important than income in the short term?

d) How big a risk, if any, are you prepared to take?

e) How far do you trust your own judgement?

f) Would you prefer to trust the judgement of professional investment managers? (If so choose a unit or investment trust.)

Examples

Inflation proofed	Index-linked National Savings Certificates Index-linked gilts bought on issue and kept until maturity.
Not inflation proofed but return of capital guaranteed	Bank deposits. Building society investments. Ordinary National Savings Certificates. National Savings Yearly Plan. Local authority loans. Most pensions and insurance (except unit-linked).
Some risk of losing capital	Local authority stocks. Gilts.
More risk	Unit and investment trusts. Stocks and shares. Property.
High risk	Commodities. Gold. Offshore trusts.

4. Do any limits on different kinds of investment apply to you?

Generally speaking, if you are over 18 and have the cash you can invest in any of the schemes discussed in Part One. But there are some limits.

The first of these is economic: many of the most profitable investments insist on a minimum sum. Even when there is no minimum, the cost of dealing in some types of investment in small amounts makes it not worth your while – for example, if it costs you £105 to buy £100 of stock paying 8 per cent you could end up with a profit of 3 per cent in the year.

Another major limitation is administrative. If a scheme is very advantageous for taxpayers there may be an upper limit, as in most National Savings schemes. Many other investment plans impose a maximum so they don't get swamped by one or two big holdings that could cause instability if, for instance, they were suddenly withdrawn.

The third and perhaps most important limitation for the small investor is the availability of tax concessions. Many investment plans calculate their rate of return on the assumption that you are entitled to the tax relief permitted by the government. If you exceed the amount allowed, you lose the tax relief which cuts down your profit correspondingly. So the two questions you have to ask yourself are:

a) Do I have enough to invest in that kind of investment?

b) Have I already put in the maximum allowed?

Examples	
Low (or no) minimum deposit	Bank deposits. Building society ordinary shares. National Savings Certificates. National Savings Investment accounts. Various regular savings plans.
£500-£1000	Some local authority loans. Yearling Bonds. Some single premium insurance policies. Business Expansion Scheme.
£5000 plus	National Savings Income Bonds. Many other income bonds. Some forestry trusts. Currency funds. Portfolio with good spread of shares.
Tax concessions	
Personal pension plans	Relief at highest rate of tax up to 17½ per cent of *relevant* income.
Employer's pension	Up to 15 per cent of earnings.
Friendly society insurance linked investments.	You can contribute a maximum of £10 a month to friendly society schemes.

5. How much time do you want to spend on your portfolio?

There are two extremes here: the person who turns investing into a consuming passion, reads the FT from cover to cover before breakfast, and a dozen other media reports every week, tunes into teletext every hour to see how the market is doing and is constantly switching from one investment to another; and the person who decides to leave it all in the bank and forget about it.

Without going in for 'churning' your money over and over, which is likely to be more profitable to your stockbroker than to you, it's a pity not to take some interest in how your money is doing. It can be a fascinating hobby, as well as a profitable one, and stagnation never did anything any good, least of all money.

Here are some questions to sort out whether you are an active or a passive investor.

a) How often are you prepared to review your investments:
   Once a week?
   Once a month?
   Once a year?
   Less often?

b) How prepared are you to take an interest in the financial scene:
   By reading the financial press daily/weekly/monthly?
   By listening to daily financial reports on the radio?
   By going to courses and conferences on financial affairs?

c) Do you mind paying the cost of switching unit trusts or commission to stockbrokers in the hope of extra profits?

d) Do you want to investigate the moral and political dimension of your holdings?
   Would you object to shares in South African companies, arms manufacturers, or gambling clubs, for example?

e) Are you a tortoise or a hare in your investment policy? Tortoises can afford to take things slowly; hares have to keep one jump ahead.

6. What kind of return are you looking for?

It's no good saying that what you want is a high rate of interest plus a large increase in the value of your capital when you cash it in. You have to make up your mind which is more important, or compromise. Broadly speaking, investments that pay above average rates, such as local authority loans, will not increase the value of your capital, unless you re-invest the interest as you go along. Investments like life insurance and pensions, whose purpose is to increase your capital, pay no interest at all. Many investment plans, especially unit trusts, aim at the compromise – some capital growth and some income.

You can go for short-term capital gains, but these investments are always likely to be speculative; some you win, some you lose.

a) Do you want a high income rather than an increased lump sum on repayment?

Examples
National Savings Investment account.
Some income bonds.

Local authority loans.
Building society extra interest accounts.

b) Do you want a guaranteed income?

Examples
Local authority loans.
Other corporation loans.
Gilt-edged securities.
Some income bonds.
Annuities.

c) Do you prefer to be fairly sure of a large capital sum at the end of
the investment term rather than high rates of interest?

Examples
National Savings Certificates.
With-profits endowment insurance.
Unit-linked savings plans and life insurance (some risks involved).

d) Do you want to know in advance exactly what the return will be?

Examples
Fixed-interest fixed-term investments such as gilts, loans kept until
maturity.
Guaranteed value life insurance policies.
National Savings Yearly Plan.
National Savings Certificates.

e) Do you want a regular tax-free income?

Examples
For basic rate taxpayers, building society investments and some single
premium life insurance schemes.
For higher rate taxpayers, a planned sequence of National Savings
Certificates cashed in year by year.

f) Do you hope for both interest and capital growth?

Examples
Many unit and investment trusts if you accept the risks involved.
Shares in sound and profitable companies.

g) Do you hope for capital gains in the short term, rather than
income, and don't mind taking risks?

Examples
Buying and selling stocks and shares.
Trading in options.
Gambling on the IG Index.
Recovery trusts.
Commodities futures.

h) Do you hope for capital gains in the long term and don't mind
taking risks?

Examples
Unit trusts offering capital growth.
Gold.
Antiques.
Property.
Stocks and shares.
The Unlisted Securities Market.
Small business.

7. How much tax do you pay?

Many investors are so anxious not to pay more tax than they need
that they refuse to manage their investments so as to get the best
out of them: 'Why should I bother when it all goes to the tax
man?' they complain. The fact is that there are anomalies in the
tax system by which people on very low incomes (around supple-
mentary benefit level) or state pensions can pay large amounts of
tax on a small increase in earned income. But the majority of
people with a little money to invest don't pay more than 40 per
cent tax at the outside. Even if you pay 60 per cent tax you are still
better off by using your money productively.

To put it another way, £1000 in an ordinary bank deposit
account at 6 per cent pays £60 a year. £1000 in a high interest bank
loan paying 8.75 per cent gives you £87.50 a year, almost 46 per
cent more. Taxed at 60 per cent you get £37.80 from the first,
£52.20 from the second. Which would you rather have?

It is when you are at or near a tax threshold that you need to
take particular care. If you are almost up to the limit above which
a higher tax rate is payable, it may be sensible to look at tax-free
investments, or for capital gains rather than income. If you are
getting near the maximum allowed for untaxed capital gains, it
may be sensible to delay selling an investment until the next tax
year. Note the 'may'. It all depends on circumstances. The questions deal with the tax dimension of investments; there will be
other factors to take into account, such as accessibility etc.

a) Do you and your family have the maximum in tax-free investments?

   If not, is the net return you are getting (after capital gains tax and
   income tax) from other investments better than it would be from
   tax-free investments?

b) Are you taking full advantage of tax concessions?

   If not, is the return you are getting from other investments better
   than it would be from investment using these concessions?

c) Is your income near the top of one tax band?

   If so, will 'grossing up' of tax-paid investments push you into a higher tax bracket?

d) Have you almost used up your allowance of untaxed capital gains?

   If so, have you explored all the possibilities of turning capital gains into tax-free investments?

e) Would you be better off paying CGT at 30 per cent (1986) than getting extra income on which you might have to pay tax above the basic rate?

Examples
Investments free of all tax
National Savings Certificates.
Gains from regular premium life insurance policies lasting more than ten years.
Premium Bond wins.
IG Index wins.

Investments free of capital gains tax
Gilt-edged securities.
Gains from single premium life insurance policies (income tax instead).
Gains from pension plans.
Antiques and jewellery valued at under £3000.

What to put in your basket of nest eggs

It may be futile to give advice in a book; nevertheless here are some suggestions for a basket of basic provisions that small investors might want in their store cupboard.

1. *Index-linked gilts*
   Preferably bought at issue, certainly not at a price higher than maturity value, and must be kept for more than a year.

2. *National Savings Investment account*
   Because it pays a good rate of interest and is easily accessible.

3. *Ten-year regular payment life insurance policy*
   For security and long-term saving. Good for providing for children.

4. *Personal pension plan*
   Essential for the self-employed.

5. *Unit trust savings plan*
   To participate in the stock market at lower risk.

6. *A small business loan*
   To support home-grown products.

And for jam:

7. *A dabble in traded options*
   All the fun of the stock market at less cost.
8. *A few gold coins; a piece of good furniture or china; a share in a forest*
   For personal satisfaction and long-term growth.
9. *A few shares in Rothschild's Old Court Fund*
   To give some international flavour.

Where to find out more

Adult education
Most local education authorities sponsor day and evening courses in personal investment and other financial topics. Well worth trying.

Chambers of Commerce
Your local Chamber of Commerce may offer conferences and day courses on investment or run an Investors' Circle.

Publications
Banks, big accountancy firms, the Stock Exchange, and trade associations may all have extensive lists of publications, many of which are free to customers or members. Write to the head office for details, or ask at the local branch. A forthcoming book, *Sources of Free Business Information* (Kogan Page) lists many of these companies. Peat Marwick Mitchell & Company, for example, offer publications on taxation, accounting, banking and investments. These include investment guides for every major industrialised country, and are free to customers, £1 each to outsiders, from the Professional Practice Department at 1 Puddle Dock, London EC4V 3PD; tel: 01-236 8000.

A visit to the local public library will show you just how many books there are on investment in general and on specialised topics.

Useful addresses

Age Concern, 60 Pitcairn Road, Mitcham, Surrey CR4 3LL; tel: 01-640 5431

Arthur Andersen and Company, 1 Surrey Street, London WC2R 2PS; tel: 01-836 1200

Association of Investment Trust Companies, Park House, 16 Finsbury Circus, London EC2M 7JJ; tel: 01-588 5347

Banking Information Service, 10 Lombard Street, London EC3V 9AP; tel: 01-626 8486

British Insurance Association, Aldermary House, Queen Street, London EC4N 1TU; tel: 01-248 4477

British Insurance Brokers Association, 10 Bevis Marks, London EC3A 7NT; tel: 01-623 9043

British Property Timeshare Association, The Secretary, Westminster Bank Chambers, Market Hill, Sudbury, Suffolk CO10 6EN; tel: 0787 310 749

Building Societies' Association, 3 Savile Row, London W1X 1AF; tel: 01-437 0655

Capital Taxes Office:
England and Wales: Minford House, Rockley Road, London W14 0DF

Scotland: 16 Picardy Place, Edinburgh EH1 3NB

Northern Ireland: Law Courts Building, Chichester Street, Belfast BT1 3NU

Chartered Institute of Public Finance and Accountancy, 65 London Wall, London EC2M 5TU; tel: 01-638 6361

Children's Legal Centre, 20-21 Compton Terrace, London N1 2UN; tel: 01-359 6251

Finance Houses Association, 18 Upper Grosvenor Street, London W1X 9PB; tel: 01-491 2783

Financial Times Business Publishing Ltd, Greystoke House, Fetter Lane, London EC4A 1ND; tel: 01-405 6969

Forestry Investment Management, Barrington Farmhouse, Great Barrington, Burford, Oxon OX8 4US; tel: Windrush (04514) 322

IG Index, 9-11 Grosvenor Gardens, London SW1 0BD; tel: 01-828 5699

International Gold Corporation, Wool House, 6 Carlton House Terrace, London SW1Y 5AE; tel: 01-930 5171

Life Offices Association, Aldermary House, 10-15 Queen Street, London EC4N 1TP; tel: 01-248 4477

London Enterprise Agency, 69 Cannon Street, London EC4N 5AB; tel: 01-236 2676

London International Financial Futures Exchange, Royal Exchange Building, London EC3V 3PJ

National Association of Pension Funds, Prudential House, Wellesley Road, Croydon CR9 9XY; tel: 01-681 2017

National Association of Securities Dealers and Investment Managers (NASDIM), 27-28 Lovat Lane, London EC3R 8EB; tel: 01-283 4818

National Girobank Headquarters, Bootle, Merseyside G1R 0AA; tel: 051-928 8181

National Savings Bank Headquarters, Glasgow G58 1SB

National Savings Certificate Office, Durham DH99 1NS

National Savings Premium Bonds Office, Lytham St Annes, Lancashire FY0 1YN

National Savings Stock Register, Bonds and Stock Office, Blackpool, Lancashire FY3 9YP

National Union of Students, 461 Holloway Road, London N7 6LJ

Peat Marwick Mitchell & Company, Professional Practice Department, 1 Puddle Dock, London EC4V 3PD; tel: 01-236 8000

Quotel Insurance Service, GSI UK Ltd, Stanhope Road, Camberley, Surrey GU15 3PS; tel: 0276 62155

Small Firms Information Service, Dial operator on 100 and ask for freefone Enterprise. Local offices are in the telephone book.

Stock Exchange, London EC2N 1HP; tel: 01-588 2355

Trustee Savings Bank Central Board, 25 Milk Street, London EC2V 8LU; tel: 01-606 7070

Unit Trust Association, Park House, 16 Finsbury Circus, London EC2M 7JP; tel: 01-628 0871

Which?, 1 Caxton Hill, Hertford SG13 7LZ; tel: Hertford (0992) 57773

Index

Main entries are shown in italics.

Abroad, investing *141*
  living abroad after retirement 152
Account (Stock Exchange) 59
Accountants (as advisers) 177
Accumulation 172
Acid test ratio 183
ACT 166
Additional Voluntary Contributions
  (AVCs) *110*
Advanced corporation tax
  (ACT) 166
Advice 174-81
Advisers *174*
Age allowance *158*
  and insurance policy gains 92, 150
Age Concern 150
Age income relief, *see* Age allowance
Alliance Building Society 33
Annuities *108*, 114
  and SAYE 99
Antiques *128*, 151
  and VAT 167
Assets *182*
Association of Investment Trust
  Companies 77, 78
Authorised share capital 184
AVCs 110

Backdating pension contributions *106*
Backwardation 184
Balance sheet *183*
Banking Ombudsman 41
Bank of England 170
Banks 36-42, 148, 151, 177
  as advisers 177
  base rate 37
  deposit accounts 38
  investment accounts 39
  large deposits 40
  National Girobank *40*

  savings accounts *38*
  Trustee Savings Bank *40*
Base rate 37
Bears 183
Betting index *137*
Bid price:
  shares 59
  unit-linked insurance 95
  unit trusts 72
Bond funds *94*
British Government stocks, *see* Gilts
British Property Timeshare
  Association 145
Building societies 27-35, 145, 148, 151
  cheque accounts 31
  deposit accounts 29
  extra interest accounts 32
  index-linking 33
  linked to life insurance 98
  Ordinary Share accounts 29
  SAYE schemes 30
  special offers 33
  subscription accounts 30
  term shares 31
  taxation 158
Building Societies Association 25
Bulls 183
Business Expansion Scheme *135*

Capital 183
Capital bonds *31*
Capital gains tax (CGT) *161*
Capital growth funds 74
Capitalisation issue *65*
Capital transfer tax, *see* Inheritance
  tax
CAR (compounded annual rate) 172
Cash and carry operation 116
Chartered Institute of Public Finance
  and Accountancy (CIPFA) 49

Chattels 152, 160
Cheque-save accounts 31, 37
Children *146*, 167
  unit trusts 71
Children's Legal Centre 149
City Business Library 181
Churning 195
Clawback 92
Close companies 136
Collectables *128*
Commercial letting 130
Commission:
  National Savings Stock Register 21
  stockbrokers' *60*
  traded options 68
Commodities *119*
  funds 122
  futures 120
Commodity trusts 75, 122
Composite rate *158*, 171
Compounded annual rate (CAR) 172
Consideration 59
Contango *184*
Contract note 59
Convertible loan stock 63
Co-operative Retail Services Ltd 51
Corporation loans/stocks 51
Corporation tax 91, 165
Coupon 45
Covenants 148, 149, 152, *167*
Cum-dividend:
  gilts 46
  shares 61
Currency *126*
  currency accounts 126
  deposit funds 127
  investing abroad 141
  managed funds 127

Daily Telegraph 179
Debentures 62
Deposit accounts:
  bank 38
  building society 29
  currency 126, 127
Deposit administration schemes 107
Deposit bonds 23
Deposit Protection Board 36
Diamond bond schemes 125
Diamonds *124*
Discount 185
Distribution 73

Dividend 46, 60, *169*
Double taxation agreement 142

Economist 179
Endowment insurance *93*
Equitable Life Assurance Society 111
Equities *63*
Equity financing 134
Eurobonds *144*
Eurocurrency 144
Ex-dividend:
  gilts 46
  shares 61
Extel cards 181
Extra-interest accounts *32*

Family bonds *98*
Finance house loans *51*, 54
Finance Houses Association 51
Financial advice 175-80
Financial companies (as advisers) 178
Financial jargon 182-7
Financial press *178*
Financial Services Bill 181
Financial Times 28, 66, 75, 81, 84,
  104, 120, 125
  indices 178, 186
Fixed interest stocks, *see also*
  Gilts *62*
Flexible endowment policies 94
Flexible pension plans 107
Foreign banks 144
Foreign currency *126*
Foreign government stocks 143
Fountain Forestry 133
Framlington Trust 75
Franked income *166*
Friendly societies:
  bond schemes *98*
  Chief Registrar 27, 88
  insurance 88
Futures 116-40
  commodities 120
  gold 124
  IG Index *137*

Gearing 185
Gems *124*
Gifts:
  and capital gains tax 160
  and covenants 168-9
  and inheritance tax 163
Gilt-edged securities, *see* Gilts

Gilts 43-8, 53, 54, 148, 151
  fixed-interest stocks 62
  index-linked stocks 47
  issues 44
  National Savings Stock Register
    20-21
Gold *122*
  bullion 123
  coins 123
  funds 124
  futures 124
  IG Index 137
Government stocks 43-56; *see also*
  Gilts
    foreign government stocks 144
Granny bonds, *see* National Savings
  index-linked savings certificates
    building society 34
Grossing up tax 158
Growth bonds *97*
Guaranteed income bonds *97*
Guaranteed interest rates 33, 170
Guardian 179

Habitat 64
Hedging 185
Henderson Oil and Natural
  Resources Trust 122
High income trusts 74
High Street banks 36-42
Holiday letting 130
Home income plans *131*
Home ownership 129

IG Index *137*
Income bonds:
  building societies *31*
  insurance 92, 100
  National Savings *22*, 25
Income tax *155*
  children 147
  rates 156
Index-linking *185*
  building societies 33
  capital gains tax 162
  gilts 47
  insurance 99
  National Savings Certificates 17-18
  National Savings indexed income
    bonds 22
  SAYE 16
Indices *186*

Financial Times 178
IG Index 137
Industrial and Commercial Finance
  Corporation (ICFC) 134
Inheritance tax *163-5*
Insurance 88-105
Insurance brokers 89, 177
Insurance Brokers Registration
  Council 89, 197
Interest 169-74
  effect of tax 172
  guarantees 170
  interest rates 169
  loss of interest 171
Interest relief scheme *136*
International Gold Corporation 123
Investing abroad *141*
Investing for children *146*
Investing for over 65s *149*
Investment account:
  banks *39*
  National Savings 15, 24
Investment advisers *175*
Investment bonds *94*
Investment consultants 177
Investment diamonds *125*
Investment income surcharge 156
Investment trusts *76*, *86*, 122, 144
  unit trusts 70
Investor Protection Bill 181
Investors Chronicle 179
Investors in Industry (3i) 51
Issues:
  capitalisation/scrip/bonus *65*
  equities *63*
  gilts *43*, 44
  National Savings 13
  rights *65*

Jobbers 57

Kellaway, L 66
Keynes, John Maynard 122
Krugerrands 123

Lender of last resort 150
Letting 130
Liabilities 182
Libraries *180*
Licensed dealers 176
Life insurance 88-101, 148, 151
  building society linked 98
  endowment policies 93

income bonds 97
insurance brokers 89, 177
premium subsidy 90
top-slicing relief *90*
unit-linked schemes 94
variable life plans 94
whole life schemes 93
Limited editions 129
Liquidity 186
liquidity ratio 187
Listed companies 63
Loanback *111*
Loans 43-56
local authority stocks 48
negotiable bonds 50
Town Hall bonds 49
yearling bonds 50
London Enterprise Agency (LEntA) 135
London Gold Futures Market 123
London Gold Market 123
London International Financial Futures Exchange (LIFFE) *126*
London Options Clearing House 68
Loss of interest *171*
Lump sum SAYE 31

Managed currency funds 127
Marriage and investment income *156*
Marriage bureau (LEntA) 135
Minimum lending rate (MLR) 37
Money Management 109, 179
Money Observer 84, 179
Murray Noble Hotline 109

National Association of Securities Dealers and Investment Managers (NASDIM) 67, 176, 181
National Girobank *40*
National Savings 13-25, 148, 149, 151
Certificates 16-18, 24
Deposit Bonds 23
Income Bonds *22*, 25
Indexed Income Bonds 22
index-linked savings certificates 17-18
information service 23
investment account 15, 174
ordinary account 15, 25, 157
Premium Savings Bonds 19
SAYE 16

savings certificates 16-18, 24
Stock Register 20-21, *25*, 45, 47, 59, 61
Yearly Plan 18
National Union of Students 168
NAV, *see* Net Asset Value
Negotiable bonds 50
Net Asset Value (NAV) 78

Observer 179
Offer price:
shares 59, 64
unit-linked insurance 95
unit trusts 72
Offshore trusts 71, 74, 97, 125, 127, *144*
Open market option 107
Options:
open market 107
pensions 107
share option schemes 69
traded options *67*
Over-the-counter bonds 49
Over-the-Counter Market (OTCM) *68*, 83

Paid-up capital 184
Paid-up insurance policies 94
Par value 63
Peat, Marwick, Mitchell and Co 200
Pensions 103-115, 148, 151
additional voluntary contributions (AVCs) 110
annuities 108
backdating contributions 106
earnings rule 150
loanback 111
open market option 107
personal pension plans 103
Personal Equity Plan (PEP) 69
Physicals 116-40
Planned Savings 84, 89, 109, 180
Policy-Holders' Protection Board 88, 103, 108, 144
Portfolio 187, 195
management 176
Post Office account 15
Precious stones *124*
Preference shares 62
Premium Bonds *19*, 24
Premium subsidy 90
Prestel 180

Price-earnings ratio (PE ratio) *61*
Property *129*
   abroad *145*
   home income plans 131
   home ownership 129
   letting 129
   property funds 131

Quotel Insurance Services Ltd 109

Radio programmes 180
Rainbow funds 74
Recovery trusts 74
Redemption date 45
Redemption yield *187*
   gilts 46
   shares 61
Retail Prices Index 186
Retirement:
   investing for over 65s *149*
   pensions 103-15
Rights issue 65
Rothschild's Old Court International
   Reserves Fund 127

Save As You Earn (SAYE):
   building societies *30*
   insurance linked 99
   lump sum 31
   National Savings 18
Savings Certificates *18*
Savings plans:
   banks *38*
   building societies *30*
   insurance 95
   unit trusts *75*
   yearly plan *18*
Savings related share option
   schemes 69
Scrip issue 65
Second home 130
   and capital gains tax 162
Securities *57*
Securities and Investment Board
   (SIB) 181
Self-employed Pension Handbook
   104
Self Regulatory Organisations
   (SROs) 181
Share exchange plans 76
Share option schemes *69*
Shares 57-87
Share shops 181

Shares in foreign companies 143
Single premium pension payments
   104
Single premium policies 90, 95
Small businesses *133*
Solicitors (as advisers) 177
*Sources of Free Business
   Information* 200
Split-level trusts 80
Spread 72, 95
Stags 64
Stamp duty *166*
Standard 64
Stockbrokers *57*
   fees 60
   how to find 59
   negligence 58
Stock Exchange 57-87
   Stock Exchange Automated
      Quotation (SEAQ) 181
   Visitors' Gallery 58
Stock market 57-87
   British Government stock, *see* Gilts
   equities *63*
   fixed-interest stocks *62*
   new issues *63*
   Over-the-Counter Market *66*, 83
   stockbrokers *57*
   stock jobbers 57
   stock options 69
   traded options *67*, 82
   Unlisted Securities Market *65*, 83
Stocks 57-87; *see also* gilts
   National Savings Stock Register *20*
Striking price 64
Subscription accounts 30
Sunday Times 179
Switching:
   life insurance 97
   unit trusts 76
Syndicates (commodity) 122

Tangibles 116-40
Tapettes, taplets 45
Tap stock 44
Taxation 155-68, *198*
   and interest rates 156, 172
Tax credits 158, 173
Tax deduction certificates 173
Taxing income from property 131
Tax threshold 156
Television programmes 180

Term shares 31
Things, investment in 116-40, 149, 151
Times, The 47, 62, 74
Timeshare *145*
Top-slicing relief *91*
Town hall bonds *49*
Traded options *67*, 82
Transfer stamp duty 166
Trustee Savings Bank *40*
Trusts for children 146

Underwriting 65
Unit-linked life insurance *94*
Unit-linked pension plans *106*
Unit Trust Association 71, 75
Unit trusts *70*, 84, 122, 144, 148
  investment trusts 70
Unit Trust Yearbook 75
Unlisted Securities Market (USM) *65*, 83, 137
Unquoted trading companies 136;
  see also Unlisted Securities Market

Unsecured loanstock 62

Value Added Tax (VAT) *167*
Variable life plans 94
Venture capital schemes *136*

Which? 19, 129, 155, 180
Whole life insurance schemes 93
With-profits:
  insurance 93-4
  pensions *106*
Woodlands *132*
Working capital 184

Yearling bonds *50*
Yearly plan 18
Yield *187*
  gilts 46
  shares 61
  unit trusts 73
Your taxes and savings in retirement 150

Zero Bonds *52*